Old House
Care and Repair

ONE WEEK LOAN

Old House Care and Repair

Janet Collings

DONHEAD

First published in the United Kingdom 2002 by
Donhead Publishing
Lower Coombe
Donhead St Mary
Shaftesbury
Dorset SP7 9LY
Tel: +44 (0)1747 828422
www.donhead.com

ISBN 1 873394 61 6

A CIP catalogue record is available for this book from the British Library

Designed by Linda Reed and Associates, Shaftesbury, Dorset
Printed in Great Britain by J.H. Haynes & Co. Ltd. Sparkford, Somerset

British Library Cataloguing in Publication Data

Collings, Janet
Old house care and repair
1. Dwellings – Maintenance and repair 2. Historic buildings –
Maintenance and repair
I. Title
690.8'37'0288
ISBN 1873394616

Library of Congress Cataloguing in Publication Data
A catalog record for this book has been requested

Contents

Acknowledgements

This is a book that I have long wanted to write as each stage of my life has let me see the joys and problems of old buildings from a new angle: practical, theoretical, personal, academic, DIY., financial and professional. One's experience can never be complete but I felt it was time to share it.

I am very grateful to Bevis Claxton for providing the drawings and many of the photographs as well as for becoming absorbed by reading drafts.

The following people have very kindly read either parts or the complete original draft of this book and made useful and constructive comments: Julian Bagg, Peter Buchanan, Jonathan Clay, Jacqui Freeman, Jane Gosnell, Bob Kindred, Matthew Slocombe, Anne Westover and others. I am very grateful to them all.

I would also like to thank Jill Pearce and Dorothy Newberry at Donhead Publishing for making it happen, and Douglas Kent for making the connection in the first place.

There are very many other people who have contributed in various ways to the contents and existence of this book. I am also grateful to the buildings that I have studied, lived in and worked on which have taught me so much.

Introduction

If you own or look after an old property, whether it is in a conservation area, is a listed building, or is just historic and you would like to know how to approach its care then you will find this book helpful. For the purposes of this book, old means anything built before the 1930s – when the use of cement became widespread and changed the character of building maintenance. Regardless of the size, type or age of property the principles of conservative care are the same.

Who will benefit from this book?

If you have never been involved with looking after an old house, or have only experienced it from the perspective of mainstream conventional modern building methods, then this book will introduce ideas that challenge a number of commonly held assumptions. These ideas are not designed to make life difficult for you. They are sound, common-sense procedures rooted in centuries of experimentation and development by skilled craftsmen and women.

When you buy an old house, you are buying something very special which is as unique as any other hand-crafted antique. This book explains how to understand old buildings and the way they function. It also explains the best way to care for old houses without harming or damaging them, so that you and future generations can enjoy them.

This book introduces the old house owner not only to conservation philosophy but to legislative matters such as planning law and tax. All these areas are subject to change and interpretation, so while believed correct at the time of going to press the reader is advised to make use of the contact organisations and websites listed at the end of the book.

Conservation definitions and philosophy

A wide variety of words are used in the context of looking after old buildings. Many mean different things to different people. So for the purposes of this book the following definitions are used:

Care means looking after the house with the greatest of respect, keeping as much of the existing fabric of the house as is possible without destroying any of it unnecessarily. When carrying out repairs, retaining the maximum amount of the existing building is the most important priority, so that you pass on something of historical value for the future. This philosophy coincides very appropriately with the current emphasis on conserving the earth's natural resources. Destroying existing materials means they will then need to be replaced with new materials. Carefully looking after an old house with respect is a way to care for the environment as well, because the majority of materials that are needed to look after and repair an old house are closer to nature than highly manufactured modern materials.

Maintenance is the inspection and day-to-day care necessary to keep the house from needing unnecessary repair. Maintaining the paint finish on a window will preserve the window frame and properly maintained gutters and downpipes will not discharge water into the walls.

Repair is necessary where structural or weatherproofing elements need to be mended, or perhaps partially replaced, to ensure their ongoing structural integrity. It is desirable to carry out repairs with the minimum loss of original fabric.

Many old houses have interesting features, some obvious and some subtle. Sundials can be quite elaborate or exist as radiating scratches on a wall. Look carefully before re-decorating.

Terms that usually give out the wrong signals are:

Restoration means trying to take a building back in time to some historical date, which is unrealistic to achieve, destroying a lot of the house's fabric and real history in the process.

Renovation literally making new, often means making more than necessary repairs to an old building and destroying original fabric.

Refurbishment can often mean the wholesale gutting of a building leaving little of the original fabric when finished. The term is often used to imply breathing new life into an old building, when it really means removing much of the original fabric regardless of whether that works, and imposing modern finishes and fittings throughout.

Later in the book, I discuss the approaches necessary for the following:

Alterations are ways in which an old house is adapted to suit a modern owner's requirements. The philosophy behind these is that the original fabric and features of an old house are kept intact.

Extensions are additions to old buildings and should be of appropriate scale. Ideally, they should be carefully built to be reversible, so that if they were to be removed the original building would not be damaged.

Responsibilities of owning an old house

Ownership of a house several centuries old is really custodianship, and successful custodianship means that future generations can enjoy the house too. You will want to be remembered as the owner who cared for the house and garden rather than the one who was responsible for harming or completely neglecting it. This means keeping as much of the original fabric of the house as possible by the minimum of work necessary. Alterations that have been carried out in the past are a valid part of the house's history and if these are removed then part of the history of the house is lost.

Ironically, what does most harm to an old house is well-intentioned but inappropriate maintenance. Most people would recognise that sanding down a Georgian table and painting it white is not a good idea, yet houses are often stripped of the materials and finishes that have been vital to their survival, only to be replaced with expensive new materials which can hasten their decay.

Choosing an old house

Before you sign anything be sure to choose a house of the right size for your needs preferably without having to alter it, as there comes a point where development, that otherwise seems reasonable, is undesirable. If you prefer large rooms to live in don't buy a cottage with small rooms and then try to turn it into something it isn't.

Once you have bought your chosen house, you might save yourself some money by living in it for about a year until you know whether you can adapt to the house instead of altering it to suit you. This will help in understanding what work, if any, is essential and which features you really like and which you might otherwise have ironed-out and lost.

Understanding the qualities of an old house

Recognising which particular features of an old house are attractive is a very difficult thing to do – even for professionals. You will have seen fake olde-worlde interiors perhaps, where every exposed timber has been purposely distressed and where every wall is covered with lumpy plaster. It is likely that those walls are, however, perfectly vertical and the timbers all the same size and evenly spaced.

Then look at a real timber-framed old house. The walls are probably reasonably smooth, but gently undulating. The timbers are probably free of rough damage, but slightly irregular in size and spacing and not quite vertical or horizontal. What appeals to us about old houses is often subtle imperfection. In decorating or adapting an old house, it is all too easy to sacrifice the very subtleties that drew us to it in the first place.

Researching the history of an old house

A very good way to understand and come to terms with an old house is to find out about its architectural and social history. Speak to neighbours and anyone else who knows your house and you should be able to start piecing together its history. Maps are a useful source of information and may be able to identify what changes have taken place over the years. For example, even privies were indicated on very large-scale Ordnance Survey maps, which may be available from your City or County Records Office.

The local studies section at your library may be able to able to help and the County Record Office and local history groups may also be a source of useful information.

Weathering can add to the character of an old stone house.

Written documents generally cover the legal history of a house or information about the families who lived there. Information about former occupants can be found from census returns, electoral registers, wills and inventories. Some may be available on microfiche from your local library or at the Public Records Office.

The numerous search engines on the Internet may turn up some interesting and unexpected information and many libraries' catalogues can now be searched online.

There are books to help you research the history of your house as well as books that deal with the development of certain types of houses. There may be books available about the local vernacular traditions and styles in your area. Ask the conservation officer at your local council or contact the local studies section at the local library. There are also various books about particular types of buildings.

As well as the research you do, it is worth keeping a careful eye on what you see and find around your house and garden. A hidden fragment of stone or glass buried in the garden may later turn out to be part of their history. Keep a record of any finds and when they were found, together with photographs, so that you have a record about your house for both your benefit and for those who come after you.

1

The nature of old buildings

Care was taken when houses were first constructed to make sure that they had a good hat on them. Roofs were designed with a wide overhang to protect the walls from water running down them. Many roofs, for example, thatch, were designed without gutters, so an overhang was a vital part of the design concept.

Equally important to an old house was its boots, another important design consideration. A cob or timber-framed house needed protection from damp rising up from the ground, so a base was constructed of a drier material like stone or brick, onto which the walls were built, to isolate it from the ground.

Materials

Old houses were constructed before our recent and innovative building materials were available. Even our versions of timeless traditional materials are now subtly different. While bricks and mortar together with timber and paint are available, there are often important differences between the traditional versions and the ones stocked by the builders' merchant today.

Many more materials are available now for repair and these can create serious problems for old houses. The house owner needs to understand the differences between traditional and modern materials and the consequences of using them.

Old buildings were constructed with natural materials, usually locally available to the builders. Over hundreds of years of trial and error, the strengths and weaknesses of these materials were learned and adapted into a carefully integrated system of unwritten rules.

Traditional materials and techniques allowed any water that got into them to dry out again, in other words they allowed the house to breathe. Those building materials could also accommodate a certain amount of

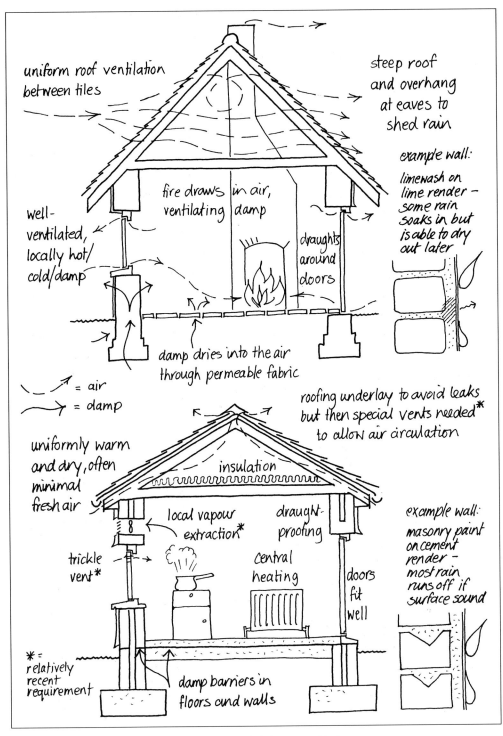

Cross-section showing: Top – How an old house was intended to cope with damp,
Bottom – How modern houses aim to eliminate damp.

structural movement without causing problems. Modern materials are often not very good at this, for example, if a hard cement render is applied to cover an older brick or stone wall, it is likely to start cracking.

The need for old buildings to breathe

Buildings constructed before the mid-nineteenth century coped without effective damp-proof courses. The reason for this is that when some water rose from the ground up the walls it was able to evaporate higher up, because breathable materials were used that allowed this process to happen without damaging them. A lot of the moisture goes in and out of the wall though the mortar joints, rather than through the stone or bricks. The result is that over a long period – maybe every hundred years or so – the mortar that has been doing most of the breathing wears out at the face of the stone or brick where most of this process happens, and has to be re-renewed. This is sometimes referred to as sacrificial mortar.

Problems start to happen in old buildings when people expect them to behave like modern buildings. Floors are sealed with damp-proof

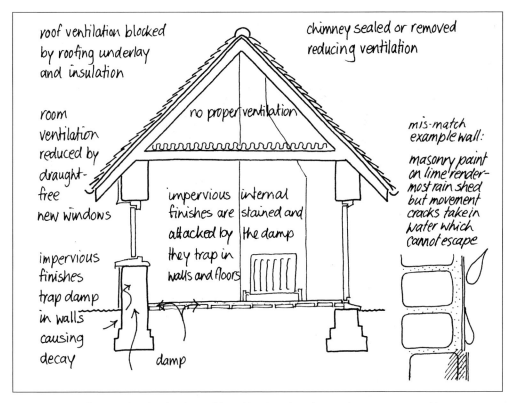

Cross-section showing how mixing old and modern damp regimes can cause problems.

membranes and walls with impervious paints and renders. Ground-water still rises of course, but it has nowhere to go, so it collects in the fabric, causing staining and decay. Not understanding quite what has happened, elaborate damp-proof courses are installed in the walls to try to stop the water rising. This technology, borrowed from use in more stable modern buildings is not always successful in old buildings.

In the worst cases fitting a damp-proof course (dpc) to an old property retrospectively simply introduces impermeability, sealing damp in and causing further problems. It does not attempt to understand what the cause of the dampness is in the first place, so that the solution does not deal with the overall problem.

A traditionally constructed building with a breathable wall fabric, could allow moisture to dry out because the lime-based renders and paint finishes were generally permeable. But once the modern builder and decorator have unknowingly sealed everything up in relatively brittle cement render and plastic paint, then tiny cracks can form and minor leaks collect in the fabric where they can cause rot and decay.

Decay caused by a combination of ground water rising up through the soft bricks (because it has nowhere else to go) and rain-splash from the hard surface. Damp collects above the cement plinth and in winter this freezes, crumbling the bricks.

Old buildings move

Modern buildings are designed to be rigid, so most conventional modern materials need not allow for deformation. Most movement is restricted to carefully designed movement joints. On an old building, there are usually no specific movement joints because every part of the structure tolerates slight movement. Walls that move on simple foundations, as they were intended to do, may crack and admit small amounts of water. Traditional materials permit drying out.

Where an existing brick or stone wall has been rendered with a cement render or if it has been painted with a plastic paint, then once water gets into a crack its only way out is back through the crack. Water is unlikely to find the same route back out again through a tiny crack, so there it stays.

Further back in history when heating came from a fire in the middle of the floor and windows had no glass (and quite a few of our surviving old buildings started out this way), then the fact that a gap opened up in a wall from time to time was not a serious problem. Now it is, and over the centuries these buildings have slowly been refined and clad and glazed to keep out more and more of the weather and keep in more and more of the heating. But they still move. When the whole structure is knitted together with compatible materials, they all move together and accommodate movement within the structure. These old buildings need a material to accommodate movement and allow water to dry out again. There is such a versatile material and it is lime.

Left – This window seems to have settled without causing serious cracking because the wall was constructed using lime mortar which tolerates some movement (the glass will almost certainly have been replaced over the years).

Below – Lime in this crinkle-crankle wall mortar does not need elaborate movement joints.

traditional materials (eg lime mortar/render, limewash) are relatively tolerant of movement

if a traditional lime render/ limewash finish cracks, water getting in can dry out through the finish

old houses used simple foundations - so the rest of the structure had to be able to cope with movement

many old houses were built with natural materials which move with the seasons or over time - so doors and windows needed to be adjustable

modern materials (eg cement mortar/ render, plastic paint) perform well if movement is minimal

if surfaces are stable and do not crack, the relatively waterproof properties of cement render can keep modern walls dry

modern houses use stable concrete foundations, perhaps quite deep, to minimise ground movement

rigid walls permit the use of less adjustable materials for doors and windows

Top – Old houses aimed to cope with movement,
Bottom – Modern houses aim to eliminate movement.

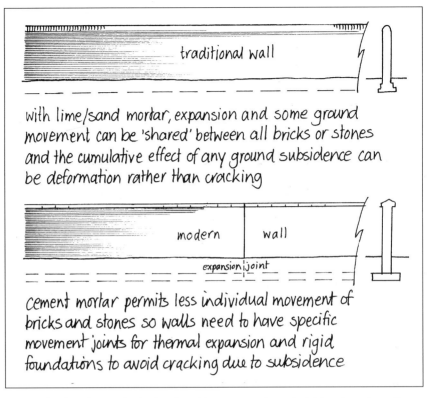

Traditional and modern methods of coping with movement shown by brickwork garden walls.

Lime

Lime mixed with sand has been a universal material used in mortars to bed bricks and stone and also for plastering ceilings and both masonry and timber walls for thousands of years. Cement (modern Portland cement invented in the mid-nineteenth century for use in demanding engineering projects), made inroads into general building from about a century ago and, from being an additive to lime mortar mixes, often became the principal component by the last half of the twentieth century. However lime has been making a comeback in work to old buildings over the past decades as its intrinsic gentle qualities have once again been understood and valued.

Lime is made by burning limestone in a lime-kiln and the end product, after mixing the resulting quicklime with water, is a caustic white yoghurt-looking substance called lime putty.

As well as being mixed with sand to make mortars and plasters, lime putty can be diluted with water to make a useful wall finish, called

, which can be coloured with natural pigments. Lime materials have enormous advantage for old buildings. They are vapour-permeable, allowing water to dry out at broadly similar rates to most natural building stones, bricks and timbers. They are also inherently flexible, not elastic so much as having the ability to move with the building. However, importantly, if cracks occur any water getting in can still dry out. Lime products are susceptible to frost until set and should not be used externally in late autumn or winter. Lime putty is caustic and care needs to be taken in use, especially to protect the eyes. The Appendix provides fuller details of the different types of lime available today and its uses.

Why did cement supplant lime in conventional modern building? Using lime mortars is not quite so predictable as modern-day cement – there is a certain amount of skill involved to judge the mix and set of lime, whereas cement conforms better to formulae. Lime products take a long time to harden fully. Cement, on the other hand, can be guaranteed to cure in days and weeks rather than weeks and months, and will often tolerate chemical anti-freeze additives. Cement has also won a universal modern building-site presence by its parallel use in foundations and structural reinforced concrete. It is less caustic in its prepared state than lime putty and is adaptable to mechanised processes.

Nevertheless, cement is now considered by conservationists as much too strong for use with natural and traditional building materials, and its relative impermeability to water introduces a barrier to water vapour that is at odds with traditional construction. For these reasons cement can be shown, in countless examples up and down the country, to have caused real harm where it has been introduced in repairs to many old buildings.

Why is lime mortar so good for old buildings?

Take a brick or a stone wall set in lime mortar. If the ground moves slightly or the wall expands in the sun, the mortar settles a little and then it can move back again afterwards. This cycle is repeated on a daily and seasonal basis. Provided the movement is reasonably uniform, the lime-mortar wall can accommodate this without cracking.

Take the same wall in lime mortar and subject it to wet and frosty winters. Rain soaks into the wall but the moisture can pass freely through the bricks or stones and mortar and uniformly dries out again.

As the mortar is slightly weaker than the surrounding bricks or stones, moisture will tend to lodge longer in the mortar and when it freezes the mortar will suffer the frost damage rather that the bricks or the stones. The mortar, after all, can be replaced without destroying the wall. It is the sacrificial element in the wall.

And cement?

If the same bricks or stones had been set in a cement rich mortar – which is a relatively inflexible and impervious material – then the mortar would have been less able to accommodate the expansion or ground movement. As a result, both the mortar and the bricks or stones could have cracked. Once cracks develop, moisture is able to get deep into the fabric of the building and the water is unable to dry out again sufficiently. When there is rain the wall soaks up the water but a hard cement-mortar does not allow it to evaporate, trapping it in the bricks or stones. When the winter frosts arrive, the water freezes, expands, and stresses the fabric, causing the bricks or stones and the surrounding cement mortar to crack further, perpetuating the cycle of destruction.

Even without cracking taking place, soft bricks or stones surrounded by hard, rigid mortar are likely to be damaged because of that mortar. If there is slight movement, the harder mortar rubs against the softer bricks or stones. The bricks and stones have become the sacrificial element but of course, they cannot be replaced except by destroying the wall.

2

Legal responsibilities of ownership

To protect our wonderfully varied built heritage, the government in 1947 passed the Town and County Planning Act to provide the power to produce a list of individual buildings according to architectural and historic interest which were given protection from demolition, alteration or extension. These came to be known as listed buildings. Later, in 1967 under the Civic Amenities Act, the establishment of conservation areas introduced the concept of whole areas of towns or villages being given protection.

Today the principal legislation concerning listed buildings and conservation areas is consolidated in the Town and Country Planning Act 1990 and the Planning (Listed Buildings and Conservation Areas) Act 1990 in England and Wales. For Scotland this is the Town and Country Planning (Scotland) Act 1997 and the Planning (Listed Buildings and Conservation Areas) (Scotland) Act 1997, while in Northern Ireland it is the Planning (Northern Ireland) Order 1991.

A conservation area is an area of a town or village identified as being of special architectural or historical interest for which it is desirable to preserve or enhance its character. There are currently around 9,000 conservation areas in England, 600 in Scotland, 500 in Wales and 60 in Northern Ireland. Conservation areas often contain listed buildings.

If a building is designated as a listed building, it is individually identified on a list of nearly 400,000 buildings in England, just over 43,000 in Scotland, 26,000 in Wales and 8,500 in Northern Ireland. These buildings have all been selected for their architectural or historical importance.

When you purchase a house, the local authority search should usually identify if a house is listed and at what grade. The house may be in a conservation area and the search should indicate whether special designations apply such as Article 4 directions, which remove certain permitted development rights in conservation areas. These are explained later in this chapter. Other specially designated areas are national parks, areas of outstanding natural beauty and the Norfolk Broads. The local authority is usually able to tell enquirers from the address if a house is listed or is located in a specially designated area.

Conservation areas

There are many different kinds and sizes of conservation areas. While most are centred around listed or historic buildings, they can also be created where there are groups of buildings, open spaces, trees or historic street patterns, or where there is, for example, a village green or other features of historic or architectural interest.

Conservation area status means that additional planning protection is in place so that unsympathetic developments, which might otherwise spoil an area's special character, may be avoided. In considering whether to grant planning permission, there is a statutory duty to have regard to the special historic or architectural character and appearance of a conservation area, this does not apply outside a conservation area.

What does living in a conservation area really mean? It means that you may have to apply for planning or conservation area consent for work that may not necessarily need consent if it were taking place elsewhere. Most trees in conservation areas are also given special legal protection (see Chapter 10), because they can provide important visual support to the built environment.

Listed buildings have the same level of protection, whether they are inside a conservation area or not, since listed building consent for alterations is usually necessary. Trees within a conservation area are protected, whereas outside a conservation area, trees associated with a listed building might not specifically be protected unless tree preservation orders are in place (see Chapter 10).

Permitted development rights

Under current planning legislation certain types of minor changes can be carried out to unlisted houses without the need to apply for planning permission and these are called permitted development rights. Within a conservation area certain permitted development rights are reduced, so that planning permission is necessary for work which may not require planning permission outside a conservation area.

Where buildings are in multiple occupation, such as flats, or in non-residential use, they are covered by separate legislation and have fewer permitted development rights than single-family occupied houses.

Article 4 directions

An Article 4 direction means that certain permitted development rights within the conservation area have been withdrawn. These directions may vary between conservation areas according to what are the perceived threats in each area.

Article 4 directions are made when the character of an area of acknowledged importance would be threatened, and these are a means of conserving its existing character by avoiding unsympathetic alterations to unlisted single-family dwellings, which are not covered by other planning legislation, within conservation areas.

Retaining the character of conservation areas

It is often the smaller changes in a conservation area that can affect its character, so alterations and repairs should not involve the removal of existing architectural features. Any necessary repairs should be carried out using matching material and designs.

Listed buildings

What does this mean? If the house is in England and has been identified to be of special architectural or historic interest, it will have been placed on a list that is currently the responsibility of the Secretary of State for Culture, Media and Sport. A copy of the house's listing can be obtained from the local planning department, county council offices or local reference libraries. The full list is held by English Heritage at the National Monuments Record Centre at Swindon in Wiltshire.

In Scotland, the full list is held by Historic Scotland, while in Wales it is Cadw and in Northern Ireland it is the Environment and Heritage Service of the Department for the Environment for Northern Ireland.

The fact that the house is listed should usually be notified to you as a result of the local authority search when buying a house, if you were not already aware of this. When you have obtained a copy of the house's listing you will see that there is a general description of the house. This description is used for broad identification purposes only and does not provide a complete catalogue of all the features. Regardless of whether a feature is specifically mentioned in the listing description, it is still protected by listed building status. Therefore, a fireplace, for example, cannot be removed or altered without listed building consent whether it is specifically identified or not.

The house will be identified with a grade of listing. In England 92% of listed buildings are listed Grade II, with 6% listed as Grade II*, and 2% listed as Grade I. Grade II buildings are of special interest and every effort must be made to preserve them. Grade II* are particularly important buildings of more than special interest and Grade I are of exceptional interest. The majority of buildings before 1700, which have not been significantly altered since they were built, are included. Most buildings built between 1700 and 1840 that also remain in their original condition are also listed. Because so many buildings were built after 1840, and the majority of them still exist, the criteria for listing from 1840 onwards becomes more exacting.

Buildings that are just 30 years old can now also be listed, and even outstanding buildings that are over ten years old can be listed if there is a serious or immediate threat to them. Photographs are currently being

This building has existed for over 800 years; many old houses date back several centuries. Their survival proves the durability and adaptability of traditional construction.

taken of all England's listed buildings and these are being made available on the Images of England website.

In Scotland, there are about 43,000 listed buildings with categories instead of grades. Category C(s), B and A listings and the proportions of buildings in each sector are different from England, 32% are listed as Category C(s), 60% as Category B and 8% as Category A. The lists are available online at Historic Scotland's website.

In Wales there are about 26,000 listed buildings and the same system of grades are used as in England with the following percentages: 91% listed as Grade II, 6% as Grade II* and 2% as Grade I. Others, such as churches being re-classified, currently account for 1%.

In Northern Ireland, there are approximately 8,500 listed buildings. A different grading system is in operation there with percentages as follows: 95% are listed as Grade B (1 and 2), 3% as Grade B+ and 2% as Grade A.

Other special categories for consent

There are other special designations, such as areas of outstanding natural beauty (AONB) or national parks. These have their own special requirements; ask the local or park authority for details.

A scheduled monument is identified as having been put on the schedule and covers a wide range of usually unoccupied buildings or sites, from pre-historic standing stones and burial mounds to Roman forts and wartime pill-boxes. In England, applications are made to the Department for Culture, Media and Sport (DCMS). If approval is granted this is done by the Secretary of State rather than the local authority. In Scotland and Wales applications are made to the National Assemblies, and in Northern Ireland to the Environment and Heritage Service of the Department of the Environment.

Development plans

When considering a planning application, the planning and conservation officers will consider it in the light of the policies within the local authority's unitary development plan in urban areas or in other, usually rural, areas the local plan and county structure plan. These documents will identify conservation areas and indicate the authority's policies towards conservation areas and listed buildings. The officers will also consider an application in conjunction with the government's current guidelines and any supplementary planning guidance, before making their decision.

When is conservation area consent necessary?

Conservation area consent is necessary for demolishing a building with a volume of more that 115 cubic metres (there are a few exceptions). Permission would also be necessary to demolish a gate, fence, wall or railing over one metre high where it is next to a highway (this includes a public footpath or a bridleway), adjacent to a public open space, or over two metres high in other locations. To be sure of interpretation, contact the planning department at the local authority.

When is listed building consent necessary?

Listed building consent is required for any alterations, demolition or extensions to a listed building or any objects or structures within its curtilage (usually the boundary) where this would affect its character as a building of special architectural or historic interest. A common mis-understanding is that only the exterior is listed. This is incorrect. Everything is listed – the interior and the exterior, whether old or very recent. Usually, buildings or objects within the curtilage of the property, if they were built before 1 July 1948, are also listed. Curtilage often means the same as the boundary of ownership but it can refer to any implied area of influence such as the former boundaries of a property, parts of which may have been previously sold.

The type of structure that may be classed as within the curtilage of a listed building is open to legal interpretation but can include garden walls, sundials, statues and dovecotes, as well as buildings whose func-tion is ancillary to the principle listed building, such as outbuildings. Consent is required, for example, for adding or removing an internal partition, as well as for larger elements such as extensions, or alterations to outbuildings within the curtilage.

As all parts of a listed building are listed, listed building consent is usually necessary where reversals are proposed of recent alterations such as re-instating replacement windows or doors, or unsympathetic later extensions. The legislation is designed to favour the preservation of listed buildings, so all applications are considered in relation to their contribution to the preservation of the building in its setting and its architectural or historical features. The process of an application for listed building consent is not intended to prevent change but to allow careful consideration to be made of the special architectural and historical features of an old building.

Detailed guidance on listed buildings for England is set out in the government's guidance policy, which is currently *Planning Policy Guidance Note 15 (PPG 15) Planning and the Historic Environment.* Annex C of this document gives detailed guidance on alterations to listed buildings. This can be downloaded from the government's website (ODPM – Office of the Deputy Prime Minister). At the time of writing, there are discussions about replacing PPG 15.

In Scotland, the guidance is far more detailed and is contained within the *Memorandum of Guidance on Listed Buildings and Conservation Areas* (Revised 1998). In Wales, the comparable document is Circular 61/96 *Planning and the Historic Environment: Historic Buildings and Conservation Areas.* In Northern Ireland, the relevant document is *Planning Policy Statement 6: Planning Archaeology and the Built Heritage* (March 1999).

If you are proposing to carry out any works to a listed building, discuss proposals with the conservation officer, who may be based at the local district or county council, before your plans are too far advanced. They can then see if what you are proposing are acceptable alterations and whether listed building consent would be necessary.

Where like-for-like repairs are to be carried out, providing they do not cause a loss of fabric or a change in the character of a house, then consent should not be required. However, there is a grey area in deciding when a repair has become an alteration, requiring listed building consent. For example, where a brick or stone wall needs repairs it is likely that minimal pieced-in repairs might be classed as a repair, whereas substantial repairs could be seen as altering the character of the wall, so might constitute an alteration and therefore require listed building consent.

The local authority, based on specialist conservation advice, makes the decision as to what constitutes a repair or an alteration. This advice may come from the county council's conservation officer or team (if no conservation officer is employed at district level).

Replacing recent kitchen units and bathroom fittings, providing this does not affect the historic or architectural character of a listed building, may not require listed building consent. However if in the process of

Areas where timber framing was used developed individual framing patterns, this is from central southern England.

re-fitting a kitchen or bathroom, you wish to carry out alterations, like removing a partition or opening up a chimney breast to install a range-type cooker or installing extensive service runs or extract ducts, then listed building consent would be required.

The installation of items such as satellite dishes, alarm and meter boxes and flues, to mention a few, usually require consent where they affect the character of a listed building. If you propose to re-thatch a listed house and change from one type of thatching material to another, then contact the local conservation officer to see if you will need to apply for listed building consent. Apparently innocuous changes can require consent. Changing the colour of external paintwork can require consent where it could affect the character of a listed building.

You should be aware that it is a criminal offence to carry out, or ask someone else to carry out, unauthorised work to a listed building for which consent has not been granted. The penalties can be unlimited fines, up to twelve months in prison or a combination of the two.

Listed building consent may be necessary in certain situations where a planning application is not necessary, where the works proposed by a listed building application does not constitute development, for example, an application to remove the paint from the exterior of a building.

When is planning permission necessary?

Planning permission is necessary where any part of your proposed alterations constitutes physical development or a change of use within the current definitions of planning legislation. It may be required in addition to listed building consent as well as conservation area consent. Some development is permitted without applying for planning permission but in conservation areas the amount of permitted development allowed is reduced.

Further information about what you need to apply for planning permission for can be found in *A Guide for Householders* booklet (which can be viewed on the ODPM website).

What will I get permission for?

Ask the advice of the local conservation officer, as to what is acceptable within national guidelines and the local authority's policies. The conservation officer can advise you which consents you need apply for. The usual options are listed building consent (if the house is listed), planning permission, and if demolition is involved, conservation area consent.

Many local authorities produce useful guidance documents covering topics from repairs to extensions, which are available on request or may be available to download from their websites, which give advice about old and listed buildings.

Differing opinions

The care and repair of old houses is not an exact science as every old house with its situation and circumstances is different. The same diversity of opinions may also apply to those people who are involved with old buildings. The general rule is that whenever you are in doubt about an opinion or where you are not entirely happy for whatever reason, ask for a detailed explanation. Where possible, try to get a second opinion.

Remember that the majority of old buildings are damaged from a position of well-intentioned ignorance, rather than from deliberate vandalism.

How to apply for the various types of consent

The local council will be able to supply you with the appropriate forms. A fee is attached to planning applications, which varies according to the type of the works proposed. There is currently no fee attached to an application for listed building or conservation area consent. It is usual to apply for planning and listed building or conservation area consent at the same time. Some works may require all consents at the same time. Building regulations approval may also be necessary.

The government has set targets for local councils to provide and deliver services electronically. This means that you may already be able to download application forms and guidance notes from your local council's website. At present, most application forms have to be physically submitted to the local council. While the basic format of all local authority forms is the same, there can be variations in the specific information required by different councils.

Other information that should become available online will be information on which buildings are listed and where the conservation areas are in the locality. You will also be able to find out what planning applications are being considered and make comments on them.

Appeals

If a planning application is refused, you have the right to appeal to the Secretary of State. There is a time limit of six months from the date of the refusal.

How long does it take to obtain approvals?

Planning permission, listed building and conservation area consent require public consultation and so usually take eight weeks, though queries and additional information can extend this period. When the appropriate permissions have been granted they last for five years.

When approvals are issued, conditions are usually attached. If you fail to complete or meet conditions attached to consents, they can be enforced by the local authority.

Work must not be started until all the appropriate permissions have been granted.

Building regulations' approval – what they cover and how to apply

Once the necessary planning permissions have been approved, depending on the nature of the proposals, an application for building regulations approval may also be necessary. Building regulations are designed to ensure the health and safety of people in and around buildings, to conserve fuel and power and promote equal access.

The regulation documents can be viewed and downloaded from the government (ODPM) website. These regulations are regularly updated to meet changing needs.

In Scotland, building regulations are known as building standards and can be viewed at the Scottish Executive website.

Building regulations have to be complied with (unless a waiver is granted for a particular situation) when alterations or new building works are carried out that are covered by these regulations. In the legislation that covers historic buildings – which in England is currently PPG 15 – there is provision for the building regulations to be applied flexibly, so that unacceptable damage is not caused to the fabric of a listed building.

Building control deals with building regulations applications, which is separate but frequently allied to the planning department at the local council. The application form itself may already be available to download from the relevant local council's website. Application forms and drawings have to be submitted with a plan fee that like planning applications is dependent upon the scale of the project. The statutory period for approval is five weeks, which is extendible by agreement. Once permission is granted this usually lasts for three years. Conditions can be attached to the approval and work must not start on site until approval has been granted. When the building project is on site there is a further inspection fee that covers site inspections by the building control officer.

Building regulations approval can be obtained for small works on domestic dwellings through another route known as building notices. The plan and inspection fees are paid, together with details of the costs of the works, start date and a site plan as appropriate. The building works can be started 48 hours after the council has been notified and the building works will again be inspected in the same way as with the other system. Building notices cannot be used with other types of buildings or where the works need to comply with current fire legislation, so this system is only appropriate for some small domestic projects. To use this route you have to be certain that the proposed works do comply with the building regulations as the building control officer can insist that things are changed on site that do not comply (even if built).

Sometimes requirements under the building regulations may be at odds with retaining the original fabric of an old house and, where these situations arise, a compromise can usually be negotiated which may involve a waiver to the building regulations. These negotiations may need to involve the conservation officer.

Party wall awards

If you are proposing to carry out work to any wall that you share with neighbours, whether these are house or garden walls, then a party wall agreement may be required. The Party Wall Act provides for a party wall award agreement to be made between adjoining owners and covers all structures in England and Wales. Work to a party wall, or boundary, wall that does not require any statutory permission may still require a party wall award.

The Royal Institution of Chartered Surveyors (RICS) may be able to suggest building surveyors who specialise in party wall awards in a particular area and a Party Wall Act explanatory booklet is available to view on the government's (ODPM) website.

House buying legal process

When you are going through the process of buying an old house, do make sure that you get definitive confirmation on the extent of the boundaries and who owns walls, trees, ponds and anything else that could be disputed later. It is far wiser to get these sorted out than have a dispute arise later, although old properties' deeds are not always helpful at identifying these areas of ownership. The Land Registry may be able to help.

The local authority searches should also identify what planning applications have been granted for a particular property. Remember that a new owner becomes liable for any wrongful alterations that have been carried out to a listed building by a previous owner. If these were unauthorised, you will inherit them and may have to put them right.

Restrictive covenants

Many old buildings may have restrictive covenants attached to them. These may in theory be incorporated in the purchase agreement, so make sure you identify and comply with these, if they are valid, or apply for amendments if it is appropriate and reasonable to do so.

3

Professional help, money and time-scales

Anumber of professionals can help to plan and carry out work to an old house. Starting with architects or building survey-ors, these may lead you onto structural engineers, quantity surveyors and services engineers, depending upon the size and complexity of the project. Interior designers, kitchen, conservatory and swimming pool designers may also need to be involved depending on the size and scope of the project. There are also landscape architects and garden designers who can help with planning the garden. The first point of contact with a professional may be at the house purchase stage, when a survey is commissioned.

Mortgages and surveys

If you are considering buying an old building, check that the proposed lender will be prepared to lend against an old property. If you need a mortgage to buy the house, find out from the lender if their proposed mortgage valuer is knowledgeable about old buildings. If not, ask that a surveyor who specialises in old buildings be used. The Royal Institution of Chartered Surveyors (RICS) has a list of surveyors accredited in conservation.

The reason for using a building surveyor who specialises in conservation is that any problems found can be put into perspective in terms of what is usual or to be expected in old houses, rather than comparing these with modern houses that are expected to perform to quite rigorous standards. For example, a mortgage provider may want you to solve damp by installing a damp-proof course (dpc). As will be explained in Chapter 5, an injected chemical dpc can be unsuitable for old buildings and a sympathetic surveyor many see the potential for alternatives, such as a French drain and other measures (see Chapter 4).

House purchase surveys

A basic valuation survey may be the only survey carried out on a house when it changes ownership. It is advisable to have a full condition survey carried out as this can form the basis of a future programme of repairs. Even then, much will still be covered up and you may reveal surprises later if you have work carried out. Surveyors, rather than architects, usually undertake these surveys.

Professionals and how they can help

When selecting a professional to work on the project, it is vitally important to choose someone who is knowledgeable and experienced with working on old houses and who has specialist knowledge and understanding concerning old buildings. This should avoid any irreversible damage being initiated.

Given that homeowners may only repair one house during their lifetime, it is prudent to use the experience of professionals who have done this type of work before. They should be aware of the majority of problems and pitfalls that can be associated with repairing an old house. Knowledgeable professionals may also be able to suggest cost-effective solutions to problems that those unfamiliar with old buildings may not be aware of.

There are many opinions about how to care for old buildings. This ranges from minimum intervention, where as much of the original fabric is kept as is possible (and is what this book explains and encourages), to maximum intervention where a large amount of original fabric is lost, which is at the restoration or refurbishment end of the field. Establish where the professional that you are thinking of employing stands in this spectrum.

Architects

Architects are trained to understand how people live in a building and how this interacts with the design of the building. An appropriately trained or experienced historic buildings architect additionally understands historic detailing and construction methods and can blend new work carefully with old, so it is crucial that you choose an architect with this background.

The term architect is protected by law in the UK. Practitioners who are not registered architects may not call themselves architects and therefore adopt similar-sounding titles, such as architectural designer. As with any of the professionals listed below, you can check with the professional institutes and registration bodies for professional qualifications and status.

Building surveyors

They can carry out a broadly similar role to that of an architect, however they are generally trained to be more involved in the practicalities of the building process rather than aesthetic design.

Like architects, they can provide drawings and specifications for obtaining local authority consents, competitive tenders from builders and oversee the building contract on site from start to finish. Within the Royal Institution of Chartered Surveyors is a building conservation group. Just as with architects, it is most important to seek the advice of a building surveyor who is genuinely sympathetic to old buildings.

Many elements add to the character of an old house.

Structural engineers

Any existing structural problems will usually need to be assessed by a structural engineer. If you are proposing to carry out any alterations or additions, their services are usually likely to be required. Again, a structural engineer who understands old buildings is more likely to be comfortable with existing structures and traditional methods and may be less inclined to over-design remedial work.

Other disciplines

Quantity surveyors – They deal with the financial aspects of building work and on larger projects can assist with project management.
Services engineers – Often known as M&E (mechanical and electrical) engineers. They deal with heating, plumbing, drainage and electrics.
Interior designers – They advise on interior spaces, colour schemes, curtain styles and colours, furnishings, fabrics and carpets.
Other designers – Kitchen, conservatory and swimming pool designers can be part of a design team, in conjunction with other designers, or individually, as appropriate for particular elements of a particular project. They are frequently part of the company providing these goods.

How do you select the right professionals?

With all these different disciplines, the most important thing is that the people that are chosen are experienced in understanding and working on old houses. Some professionals and contractors are very sympathetic and skilled with old buildings, others have little understanding of old buildings and honestly admit it. Some think they can handle old buildings – just like new ones. The task, as a responsible old building owner, is to select from the first group who are committed to preserving and minimising intervention.

The first person you will look for if you are considering a programme of repairs is either an architect who specialises in historic buildings (if you are concerned primarily with design, space-planning and conservative repair), or a conservation accredited building surveyor if you are concerned primarily with maintenance and conservative repair. There is some natural overlap between architects and surveyors. They would be the lead consultant and may be able to suggest other consultants where necessary for the project. This will depend on the size, complexity and nature of the problems of a particular building project.

Sometimes lists of architects who specialise in working on old buildings are kept by the conservation officer at your local authority or by the conservation team at the County Council. The Society for the Protection of Ancient Buildings (SPAB) also holds lists of architects who specialise in conserving old buildings. The architects suggested through these channels are usually known to the organisations involved.

The Royal Institute of British Architects (RIBA) Client Services will be able to provide a list of architects who have indicated to the RIBA that they are interested in working on old buildings.

The Royal Incorporation of Architects in Scotland (RIAS) has a list of architects accredited in conservation. In Wales there is the Royal Society of Architects in Wales (RSAW) and in Northern Ireland it is the Royal Society of Ulster Architects (RSUA). The Royal Institution of Chartered Surveyors (RICS) lists members accredited in building conservation.

Most professional bodies have explanatory leaflets and websites about how each professional can help you and how much their services are likely to cost.

Once you have compiled a short-list of professionals, approach each one and meet them. Ask them to bring photographs of previous projects that they have worked on to show you. Take up references, and go and look at finished projects and talk to the owners if possible. As well as their expertise and knowledge, you also have to be able to get on with them personally, as a building project can take many months or years to complete. If you are using an architect to alter or extend a house, you will be entrusting them with issues affecting your way of life. Make sure you get to meet the person who is actually going to work with you and transfer dreams into reality. This can be different from the person in charge of a project at the office whom you met at the outset.

Most professionals will have a written appointment agreement that sets out the terms and scope of their services. Understand what you are getting and what you are expected to contribute to the process. If you don't understand then get them to explain it. Be clear whether you want to be involved in all the processes or simply leave them to find ideas and solutions for you.

Professionals help select which builders or craftspeople are suitable to be put on the tender list for the work. They may also have worked with the contractors on previous projects or they may take up references for you. The professional who is working for you will normally prepare a set of tender documents, which comprise drawings and specifications and/or schedule of works, which will identify all the works that are to be priced for in the building contact.

Having selected a list of suitable builders, these are each invited to submit a competitive tender for the work. The total price has to be submitted by a pre-arranged date and time to your professional adviser. Alternatively, you may negotiate a price with a single preferred contractor. In the planning stages of any project, the architect or surveyor is working for their clients' benefit. The client becomes the employer, in contract parlance, once the building contract is in place. When the contract is on site the architect or surveyor is still expected to act as the employer's agent, but they also have to try to administer the contract fairly between the employer and the building contractor.

Choosing builders and others

Where the works are sufficiently minor not to require the services of an architect or surveyor, there are various ways of finding a builder who is experienced and knowledgeable about working on old houses. Firstly, ask the local conservation officer if they can give you the names of builders known to be familiar with working on old buildings. Many local or county councils have lists of builders who are experienced in working on old houses. National amenity societies also hold lists of builders and craftspeople and may be able to give you names of people who work in your area. Family and friends may also have suggestions of experienced builders they know.

Also, keep a look out for builders who work in the area. If the finished job looks well executed ask the owner for their opinion of the builder. However, the most important quality for anyone working on a historic old building is that they are knowledgeable and experienced in working on old buildings in a sympathetic way.

Work to old houses can be more labour-intensive than new-build work, as much of the work is usually about careful piecing-in of repairs, which can be more time consuming than building from scratch. A higher level of skill and care is required so it is important to make sure that the builders chosen have those capabilities.

When making initial contact with a prospective builder, explain what the building work entails. Ask them how familiar they are with using traditional building materials. For example, where the proposed work involves mortar mixes for pointing or plasters, ask them if they are experienced in the use of non-hydraulic lime putty.

This discussion may give you an indication of their suitability before asking for names of referees to contact, ideally ask them to include homeowners and professionals that they have worked with in the recent past. Also, establish whether the proposed time scale for the works is achievable in relation to the rest of their workload. Take up references and meet the builder face to face. When satisfied, ask them to give you a written quotation for the proposed work, rather than an estimate – which is only what it says it is.

Working on old buildings does require a particular aptitude and understanding so it is likely that you will only find a very small number of suitable builders or craftspeople from which to choose in your area. If you do ask several builders to quote for a job, as a matter of courtesy let the unsuccessful ones know once you have signed the building contract as you never know when you may need to contact the others again.

Building contracts

It is usual that all building works are carried out with a building contract in place. Where you have employed an architect or building surveyor, they would advise you of the most appropriate contract for the project. If you are co-ordinating minor building works yourself, you would be well advised to consider the *Building Contract for a Homeowner/Occupier* published by the Joint Contracts Tribunal in England and Wales. This can be purchased from the RICS, the RIBA or the RIAS in Scotland.

If you choose to employ people directly without the involvement of professionals here are a few pointers:

- Always use a written contract. These help protect both parties from misunderstanding. At the very least, agree exactly what is to be done, by when and how much it will cost and agree a system for dealing with unforeseen work.
- Always get a written quotation for a fixed price rather than an estimate and ask them to specify the work that is covered by this price.
- Get the cost broken down into as much detail as possible so you can see what you are getting and can negotiate over omissions or extras. Confirm an hourly rate and overheads for costing additional works.

- Individual builders may not need to be VAT registered as they may trade under the limit for registering. Clarify whether they are registered for VAT. If they are you will have to pay VAT.
- Confirm when the works are going to start and finish. Building works can often start late and finish late because of unavoidable problems. Confirm when the builders are going to be on site and establish if they have a good reason for not arriving one day without notice.
- Make known in writing in advance and get agreed any critical dates by which certain parts of the work have to be finished.
- Confirm the extent of the works. For example, does the cost include re-laying carpets, installing light fittings as well as cleaning up?
- Check that the builder is insured for risks to persons and to property and specifically for work to the house. This should be for an adequate amount, public liability alone is insufficient. Ask for a copy of the certificate and send it to your own insurer when you tell them about the works.

Building contracts differ from most other types of contracts that are used from day to day, in that most formal versions provide for a different amount of money to be payable if a different amount of work is necessary or if other circumstances change.

CDM Regulations – Construction (Design and Management) Regulations 1994

These are health and safety regulations, which are designed to improve safe working on construction sites. The regulations are modified in the case of works by a domestic owner-occupier. Works are currently exempt from full notification to the Health and Safety Executive (HSE) under the regulations if they are to take less than 30 days or will involve less than 500 man-hours of work on site. However, if the extent of the proposed building works is to exceed these limits, then the HSE have to be notified by the contractor.

How much will it cost?

On a larger project generally more than you thought – the impossible question to answer is exactly how much more. Traditionally in new-build contracts run by architects or surveyors there is a contingency sum of around 10%, that is included in the total price to cover unforeseen circumstances. With old properties, concealed decay or problems lurking underground can be costly without offering anything visible in return. Changes can also be expensive if design, procurement and delivery periods have to be re-worked. Try to avoid last minute changes of mind unless you have agreed this is feasible with the architect and builder.

It is prudent to have money in reserve so that you can accommodate unforeseen circumstances in case they do arise, and you may feel it wise to keep this fact to yourself.

Where a builder has quoted a fixed price for the work then, providing that there are no changes and no hidden or unexpected things happen (which they often do with old buildings), you would expect to pay the quoted price for the completed job unless you have requested extras.

Grants

Grants for repair work to old buildings can be few and far between. The criteria for eligibility can vary and even if eligible there may then only be limited funds available. Grants are not often available at the time of purchase as the purchase price is usually assumed to reflect the condition of the property. Any particular type of grant scheme may only operate for a few years, so speak to the conservation officer at the local council to see what schemes currently operate in your area.

The research and paperwork involved in applying for grants can vary considerably depending on the sums involved. Grants may take some time to be awarded and where they are awarded a usual condition is that the work must not commence until written consent has been given.

Where a building is listed Grade I or Grade II* and the works are to cost over £10,000 they may be eligible for grants from English Heritage. In London Grade II listed buildings which are on the register of buildings at risk may be eligible for grants from English Heritage under the London Grants Scheme.

While it is not possible to give an exhaustive list of grants currently available, there are grant schemes in some areas run by English Heritage in partnership with the local authority known as Heritage Economic Regeneration Schemes (HERS). These are aimed at small commercial and industrial premises, but may also include domestic dwellings in conservation areas where repair and refurbishment would contribute to the economic and social regeneration of an area. English Heritage is currently not able to give grants to Grade II listed buildings outside a conservation area.

Opportunities like this can lead anywhere between a sensitive preservation and a misunderstood romantic pastiche.

Some local councils may have a small budget which is allocated to grants for owners of listed buildings. From this budget grants are offered for the cost of repairs to historic buildings. These schemes usually have a finite budget for each year, so they usually operate on a first-come-first-served basis from the beginning of the financial year in April. The size of individual grants is likely to be quite small. The local conservation officer for your area may be able to suggest any grant-giving bodies that are specific to your local area.

Two other grants that are not related to listed buildings, but are aimed at environmental health are House Renovation Grants and Home Repairs Assistance. These grants are administered by the Environmental Health Department at your local council. These particular grants are aimed at improving living conditions, but do have eligibility criteria attached. The way in which works may have to be carried out related to either of these grants may not be particularly sensitive to an old or historic building.

Grants in Scotland, Wales and Northern Ireland operate in a similar way to those in England. The equivalent grants to those of English Heritage are administered by the grants sections of Historic Scotland, Cadw in Wales and the Environment and Heritage Service in Northern Ireland.

VAT

At the time of writing, changes to the amount of VAT chargeable are being made in respect of some old buildings (most recently in connection with works to churches in use where grants are available to cover most of the VAT costs). Further changes may well happen so check for developments with HM Customs and Excise who deal with VAT.

The current situation is that certain alterations to buildings, for which listed building consent has been granted, are zero rated for VAT purposes (although VAT at the standard rate would still be chargeable on professional fees associated with this work).

Like-for-like repair (which is usually the best method of conserving old buildings) attracts VAT at the full standard rate, currently 17½%. Many see this as encouraging the wrong attitude by offering no tax incentive for careful repair. Even where listed building consent has been granted, HM Customs and Excise may take the view that the works are not an alteration but repairs and maintenance, which would then attract VAT at the full standard rate.

Where a listed building is being repaired and some alterations are also being carried out, there may be elements of the building work that are zero rated, where listed building consent has been granted for these alterations. There will also be items of repair and maintenance work where VAT will be chargeable, so the amount of VAT payable will vary for different elements of the work.

There are several areas where the dividing line between what does attract VAT and what does not, where a listed building is concerned, may be of interest to homeowners. Where a completely new bathroom is being created, the fittings for example, may be zero rated, provided that listed building consent has been granted for creating a new bathroom. Cookers are classed as white goods by HM Customs and Excise and so are subject to VAT at the full rate. However a new kitchen range that is also used as the boiler for a newly installed central heating system may be zero rated, where listed building consent has been granted.

Where a house is to be re-wired, the replacement of the existing wiring would be standard rated, whereas any new socket or new light fitting positions might be VAT free. Where a central heating system is to be installed for the first time, this could be zero rated.

A new area of VAT legislation, called urban regeneration measures, introduced in May 2001, can apply to unlisted buildings if certain conditions are met. For example, VAT may be charged at 5% when repairing houses that have been empty for more than three years or converting flats into a house. In addition, where a property has been empty for ten years or more the owner may be able to recover the remaining 5% VAT.

Also, whether VAT is payable or can be reclaimed can depend on who owns a listed building, for example a company that is registered for VAT and owns a listed building may be able to reclaim the VAT on work in certain situations. It is worth remembering that there is a three year time limit in deciding VAT liability, so that if any discrepancies come to light during that time adjustments can be made either way.

As a levy of 17½% makes a substantial difference to the cost of a project, it is prudent to establish what the VAT liability is likely to be at the outset of a potential building contract.

HM Customs and Excise information is available from them or to download from their website. They also have a telephone advice service. There are VAT consultants who specialise in VAT in relation to old buildings or even your accountant may be able to help if this is their area of expertise. There are also grey areas where VAT may or may not be chargeable according to interpretation of the rules in a particular VAT district. The VAT office where the contractor is based will deal with the project. Sometimes a building contract may include a provision for adjustments of the sum payable by the building owner to the contractor if a ruling changes.

It may be prudent in some situations to obtain a written confirmation of the VAT liability from the VAT office at the design stage. Individual builders may not be registered for VAT if their turnover is below the lower threshold limit for charging VAT. If you find a contractor who does not have to charge VAT for their services, as well a being experienced with working on old buildings, this may be beneficial to the budget and the old house.

However do remember that the builder will still have to pay VAT on items purchased in connection with the project, such as building materials or hire charges for equipment and will have to pass this cost on to you.

By the nineteenth century, cottages began to be consciously designed to look 'vernacular'. Generally the materials and techniques used were genuinely traditional.

Can you live with a building project?

Apart from financing it you will, if you are planning to be in residence during the work, have to put up with a lot of disruption, dust and inconvenience. If the works are extensive consider temporary accommodation for the duration of the contract.

Storage of building materials

In order for the builder to carry out work to the house, they will need to store building materials and equipment near their working area. If you have a professional involved in overseeing the building project for you, they should discuss suitable storage areas with you. These may then be incorporated into the contract.

If you are organising the building contract yourself, you must agree with the builder what is stored where. Working areas require to be fenced off for the safety of your household.

Possessions

To work effectively, and without damaging things, a builder will require a clear working area. Ideally, the existing possessions in these areas must be moved.

You must agree with the builder before they arrive to start the work, what you need to have removed. It can be surprising where builders may need to go to trace a joist, a pipe, a leak or whatever – be prepared!

Protection from damage

If you have a professional involved in running the building contract on site, they usually specify in the tender documentation a level of protection to existing features, dependent on their value and vulnerability to damage. If you are organising the building works yourself, you may wish to agree a sensible level of protection before any works commence.

Vehicles can easily damage gates and gate posts or compact the soil and so damage tree roots. Surfaces where materials or skips may be stored can also be damaged. Think about the areas to be worked on and what is likely to need protecting. This includes such things as fitted carpets, which are usually either protected or removed.

Taking photographs or a video of the existing fabric before work begins is sensible so that you do have a visual record for proof if things go wrong later.

Always agree protection with the builder at the pricing stage, rather than leaving this until the damage has been done. Make sure you know where existing services such as the mains water service and overhead cables are so that they don't get accidentally damaged. When skips or removal lorries pass near or under trees, they can easily sever large branches by accident, causing long-term damage, if adequate protection is not in place (there is a British Standard that deals with tree protection). This is covered in more detail in Chapter 10.

Garden plants near any building that is to be worked on will invariably get trampled on. You have to decide whether to protect, remove or leave them to their fate.

Other considerations about building works

Building works invariably create a great deal of dust because of the processes involved. Assume that you will still be finding dust months after the builders have left. Dust sheets are, of course, essential.

Vibration is another factor of building work and can unseat anything hung on walls or on shelves. Protect or store delicate items. To protect fragile items like ceilings, you may want to ask the builder to use alternatives to hammer and nails for some carpentry work. Nail guns can reduce hammering, screws avoid it.

If any of the services (plumbing, wiring, gas, drainage) have to be altered or upgraded, there will be periods of time when you may have to be without these. Plan for these situations.

Builders will require the use of a toilet (or provide their own), a means of making tea or coffee and somewhere to eat their lunch.

Paying the builder

Pay promptly on receipt of an invoice if you are happy with the work, especially as the builder often has to outlay for materials before you pay them. This is the most important way in which you can show the builder that you really appreciate the work that they are doing.

Sorting out problems

If you are unhappy with some aspect of the builder's work, deal with the problems as they arise. Do not leave it until an invoice is presented, as neither of you will be happy.

How long will it take to complete the repair of the house?

The homeowner never really knows at the outset how long their project will take, as they have usually never done it before. If you are taking on a building in poor condition it could be as much as six years before everything is in order, but this will very much depend on what you want to do and how quickly the work can be carried out.

Set a realistic level of completion that you can live with. While the intention may be to have every detail perfectly finished, the reality is that compromises may have to be made.

Time-scales and planning

Completion dates are often missed, despite any financial penalties included in building contracts so try to leave delivery of any new furniture or carpets as flexible as possible. Programme their arrival only when the building works are completed.

Works to old buildings are best carried out between May and September each year, because lime and other water-based materials and finishes are at risk from frost.

For a reasonably complicated project, requiring the preparation of drawings and specifications an average time-scale from commissioning a professional to submitting an application to the local authority is about six to eight months.

It may take eight weeks for the local authority to approve a listed building or planning application, providing there are no objections to the application. Building regulations approval can take up to five weeks. It is usual for the architect or building surveyor to require time following planning approval to work up further technical drawings for a building regulations submission. If you are employing a professional they also prepare the tender documentation, which will vary according to the size of the proposed contract. This documentation can include a specification and/or a schedule of works together with a set of drawings.

Once all this information has been assembled and a tender list of contractors has been compiled, the tender documents are issued to the contractors for pricing. Contractors are usually given three to four weeks to price a tender, which has to be returned by a particular date to the person overseeing the project.

Even if you are negotiating a price with an individual contractor, if it is a sizeable contract, they will need a similar amount of time to obtain prices from any sub-contractors and to work out their own costs based on the materials and labour necessary.

Once the successful contractor has been selected, they will usually require a few weeks to organise the project off-site before they start work on site.

4

What causes old buildings to decay?

T wo principal reasons why old houses decay are lack of maintenance and the use of inappropriate materials to repair them
(which is covered further in the next chapter).

Lack of maintenance

Maintenance principally means preventing water from collecting where
it can do harm, since water in the wrong place sets off most building
decay. This means carrying out periodic checks to ensure that gutters,
downpipes and drains are not blocked or leaking and dealing with problems when they arise, not a year later when a large quantity of water has
got into the fabric of an old house. Dealing with small problems before
they get worse will save a lot of time, money and effort.

Roof leaks

The greatest potential for water to enter the home is through the roof.
The introduction of roofing underlay, which is placed beneath roof tiles,
was adopted as normal practice from the 1950s onwards and acts as a
second line of defence against rain. Most roofs before this date, and
some re-laid since, do not have this additional barrier.

However, it is only relatively recently that underlays have been
offered manufactured from effectively breathable materials, which allow
air to circulate in and out of roof spaces. Underlays which do not breathe
effectively can provide conditions for mould growth in a roof space if
they cut down all natural ventilation routes between tiles or slates.

Damp chimneys

Driving rain can make chimneys and their flues damp. Providing that
any water can dry out again this may not cause a long-term problem.

Where a chimney pot is unprotected from rain, water may gather in loose internal parging that has fallen off the flue lining. Parging is usually lime plaster (sometimes mixed with dung as a reinforcement) applied to the inner face of a flue as it was being constructed to make it smoke-tight.

Coal fires release chemicals in flues that degrade this mortar and over the years loose parging may fall off and collect on the ledges. If not regularly removed when the chimney is swept this parging acts like a sponge and soaks up water. This water often finds its way through an interior wall causing dramatic damp patches.

Blocked and leaking gutters and downpipes

Gutters and downpipes often become blocked with leaves and debris from the roof and once blocked, water may cascade down the wall. This infiltrates cracks in bricks, stonework or render. The saturated walls are then subject to frost action enlarging the cracks and allowing damage to masonry or timbers beneath. Once a leak has been repaired, the remaining dampness in the walls may take months to dry out, especially if shrouded in cement or impermeable paint.

Holes in the roof and a missing section of gutter speed up decay. The missing gutter allows the water to run down the face of the wall removing mortar from around the stonework in the process.

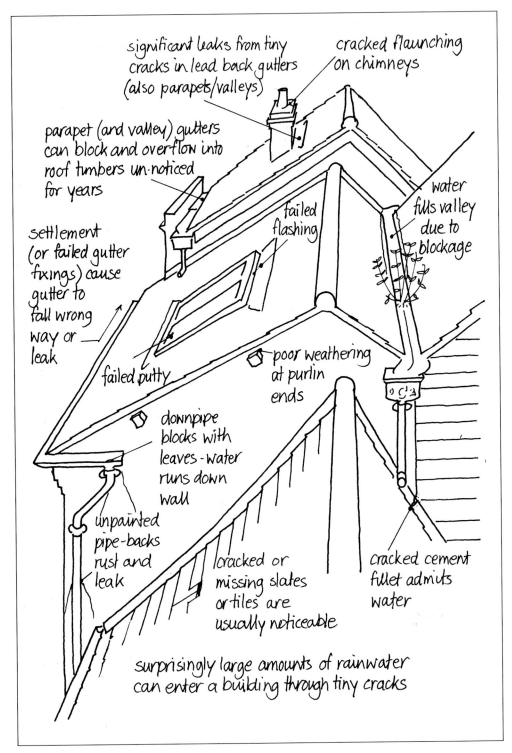

significant leaks from tiny cracks in lead back gutters (also parapets/valleys)

cracked flaunching on chimneys

parapet (and valley) gutters can block and overflow into roof timbers un-noticed for years

failed flashing

water fills valley due to blockage

settlement (or failed gutter fixings) cause gutter to fall wrong way or leak

failed putty

poor weathering at purlin ends

downpipe blocks with leaves - water runs down wall

unpainted pipe-backs rust and leak

cracked or missing slates or tiles are usually noticeable

cracked cement fillet admits water

surprisingly large amounts of rainwater can enter a building through tiny cracks

Some common causes of roof leaks (shown on a row of adjoining old houses).

Effects of driving rain

As the prevailing winter rain in the UK is usually from the south-west, this means that the effects of driving rain are most noticeable on those doors and windows facing that direction. They are a relatively smooth surface by comparison with the surrounding building fabric. Water runs down these more quickly and there are numerous joints between the timber or metal frame and the glass and putty, for water to enter direct to the interior.

Water can seep in through hairline cracks in the putty and paint around window glass to deliver a surprising amount of water. Where an external wall has been rendered or re-pointed in cement or painted with plastic masonry paint, the smallest hairline cracks allow cascading rain-water to enter the fabric of the house. Once water has penetrated cement or plastic paint it is much more difficult for it to evaporate out again.

If a lime mix has been used for the render or mortar, these materials will have settled with the surrounding materials and hairline cracks covered with each redecoration of limewash. A limewash-finished wall will temporarily absorb some rainwater so that it will not run down as freely as with a plastic-coated surface.

Moisture in the soil under and around a house

Dampness in the ground will have an effect on an old house if it is not allowed to evaporate naturally, as mentioned in Chapter 1. One method of damp management is a French drain, which helps to reduce the amount of dampness adjacent to the base of walls, see illustration (page 48) for details.

Cesspools and septic tanks

These are usually located well away from houses as they collect all the soil waste from a house where mains drainage is not available. This type of drainage is usually identified during searches connected with house purchases.

Traditionally, cesspools or cesspits were large tanks for storage of soil wastes until removed. Septic tanks are miniature sewage treatment works where the solids are broken down naturally. Reed beds are a modern re-discovery of natural water treatment using natural biological processes. These are now gaining in popularity, where space permits, and operate in a similar way in finally decaying the effluent.

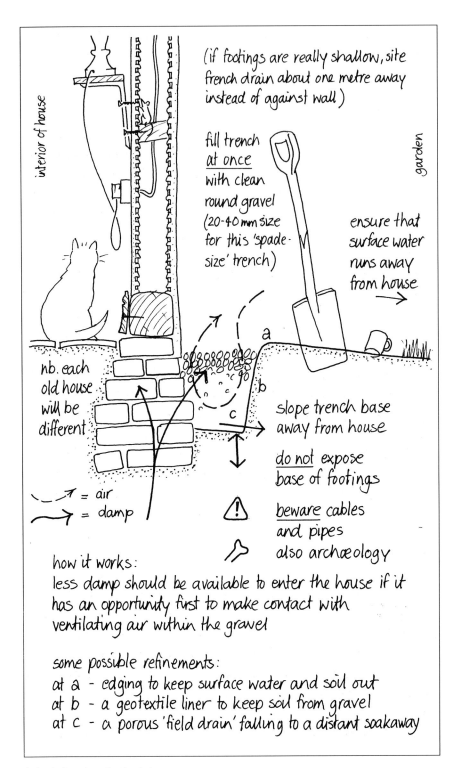

interior of house

garden

(if footings are really shallow, site french drain about one metre away instead of against wall)

fill trench at once with clean round gravel (20-40 mm size for this 'spade-size' trench)

ensure that surface water runs away from house →

a

b

c

nb. each old house will be different

slope trench base away from house

do not expose base of footings

beware cables and pipes

also archæology

↗ = air

➔ = damp

how it works:
less damp should be available to enter the house if it has an opportunity first to make contact with ventilating air within the gravel

some possible refinements:
at a - edging to keep surface water and soil out
at b - a geotextile liner to keep soil from gravel
at c - a porous 'field drain' falling to a distant soakaway

A simple French perimeter drain.

Check that pipes carrying this waste away from the house are not damaged, and beware of soggy ground or abundant weed growth around the tanks as this may indicate a problem.

Consequences of dampness in old buildings

Once higher levels of dampness get into old buildings it is an open invitation for other uninvited guests to take up residence. Water is the catalyst for both wood-boring beetles and rots to become active in timber. In broad technical terms, when the moisture content of wood gets above 15% it becomes attractive to insects. When the water content rises to above 20% this creates the ideal conditions for rots to become established.

By comparison with new buildings, joinery timber can be specified to have a moisture content of just 8% yet the installation of some other new timber elements can be specified to have a moisture content nearing 20%. However, the moisture content in the timber will change depending on the environment into which it is installed and maintained.

In order to reduce dampness in an old building ventilation must be increased both in the roof space and throughout the interior of the home. Try to make sure any steam created when cooking or by taking a bath or shower, is dispelled as quickly as possible. This will contribute to reducing the levels of dampness within an old house. Note that walls should ideally be vapour permeable inside, outside and all the way through for traditional damp management to work. You may need technical advice if the exterior is covered in impervious render, pointing or paints.

Insects and decay

The two principal insect pests in the UK that are attracted to boring the timbers in old buildings are furniture beetle (*Anobium punctatum*) sometimes referred to as woodworm, and deathwatch beetle (*Xestobium rufovillosum*). They are very adept at seeking out food sources. Deathwatch beetles can do serious damage because they are attracted to hardwoods and these are usually the structural timbers in an old house. Furniture beetles like sapwood (which is the wood nearest to the bark on a growing tree).

How do you tell which one you have got? The size of the holes that these beetles make in timber is usually the best indicator. Deathwatch beetle holes are bigger, about 2–3 mm in diameter, whereas furniture beetle holes are about 1 mm in diameter. (There are other insects pests to consider and identify depending on geographical location, but the basic principles are similar.)

Having established which type of beetle you have, the next question is whether it is an active colony of beetles, because you may be looking at twenty-year-old holes whose occupants have long gone.

Furniture beetle

With furniture beetle, look for very fine timber dust near the holes from early spring onwards. Note if it has been recently produced or if it has it been there for some time. By removing the fine dust and identifying the locations of holes you will be able to see if any more appear.

Once you have established that you have active furniture beetle, the single most important thing to do is to reduce the moisture content in the affected timbers. If these are in a piece of movable furniture then it should be taken to a drier atmosphere, so that as the wood begins to dry out it slowly becomes less attractive to the furniture beetles and their activity decreases.

If the affected timber is not movable then consider how the dampness can be reduced in the area around the affected timbers as this is the most environmentally friendly way of dealing with furniture beetle. However, take care not to dry out valuable timber too quickly otherwise it is likely to crack. This is probably the optimum way of dealing with furniture beetle from the occupant's point of view, as alternative methods of treatment usually involve the use of toxic chemicals in order to kill the woodworm and you may not wish to have such products used in the home.

Most of the timber treatments currently available to kill the furniture beetle are, by definition, toxic to insects. Where the timbers are in the process of drying out as a result of damp reducing measures, it may be appropriate to locally treat a piece of timber with a brush applied treatment for the short term, until a drier environment has been achieved. Targeting application to the affected site uses less chemicals than a blanket treatment.

Deathwatch beetles

Deathwatch beetles do not seem to be present in Scotland but elsewhere they may be active and visible between March and June, so it is only worth trying to find out if you have them during these months. Either use wax polish to fill up existing (flight) holes or paste paper over them. Anything from tissue paper to lining paper will be suitable. Then wait and see if any of the existing holes are re-used by the beetles. You may also be able to hear if you have deathwatch beetles. The noise they make sounds exactly like tapping the fingernail against a piece of wood five or so times in very quick succession. You may find them lying dead in an old building. They are about 6–9 mm in length and matt brown. However these should not be confused with a small blue/black metallic sheen beetle (*Korynetes caeruleus*) that are predators on the deathwatch beetles' larvae. Those beetles are your allies.

There are two spiders that can also help, *Tegenaria*, the sort that often find their way into baths has a longish body and long stout legs, and *Pholcus*, sometimes called the harvest spider, which has long thin legs and a small body. They both catch beetles in their webs so it is best to leave cobwebs in place between March and June to encourage these spiders to catch and eat your problems for you. These suggestions may help to reduce a residual deathwatch beetle population. The principal way of reducing a colony of deathwatch beetles is usually to reduce the general moisture content in the affected areas in order to make the timber unattractive and unsuitable to the insects. This can be a slow process. Start by making sure that water is not getting into the fabric of the house. Then, depending on the location of the colony, consider background heating in the affected areas to slowly reduce the moisture content of surrounding timbers. Take care the timbers do not dry out too quickly and crack.

Deathwatch beetles can cause significant damage if damp conditions are allowed to persist, in this case the interior of a structural roof timber had been hollowed out.

A common practice employed on old infested timbers was de-frassing. This is the removal of surface layers of timber that have been attacked by deathwatch beetles. During de-frassing much of the historical interest of a piece of timber could be lost and as a result this practice is no longer encouraged.

Trapping devices which use a light source and sticky paper to attract the insects have been developed and are more environmentally friendly than proprietary toxic pastes that can be spread on affected timbers. The theory with pastes is that if and when the deathwatch beetles emerge from their holes, they eat through the paste, which poisons them. But it is often very difficult to know which timbers to treat. The chemicals involved in these pastes may not be very pleasant to have in the home so do not be tempted to over-react to a beetle infestation. Remember that insecticides can also kill the natural predators and prevent them doing the job for you.

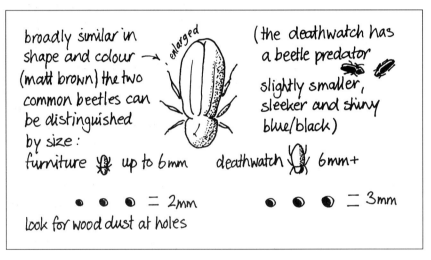

broadly similar in shape and colour → *enlarged* (matt brown) the two common beetles can be distinguished by size:

furniture ⚫ up to 6mm

(the deathwatch has a beetle predator slightly smaller, sleeker and shiny blue/black)

deathwatch ⚫ 6mm+

● ● ● = 2mm
look for wood dust at holes

● ● ● = 3mm

Two common wood-boring beetles and their flight-holes.

Rots and decay

The principal categories of rots are wet and dry, and all like damp places. It is extremely difficult to distinguish which ones you have. Even people with some knowledge find it difficult to identify dry rot from other forms of rot. All rots thrive while they have a water source. They are fungi, like mushrooms, so if you cut off their water supply they die. The length of time they take to die depends on ultimately reducing the moisture content to below the level that keeps them alive.

Rots are also extremely good at finding remote water sources. The key is to make sure there is no water getting into the house in the first place. For most rots to become established they need to have a moisture content in wood of above 20%. This has to be set against the background that all timber requires some moisture content to hang together, but when the moisture is below this level there is less likelihood of decay establishing.

What if you have rot already? Stop the water entering immediately. Then see if the rot withers. If the walls are not covered with impervious materials, a de-humidifier may be able to draw water out of the building fabric a bit faster. The success of such a strategy will vary with individual situations, especially as the rot may have remote feeding places that are impossible to access.

Identifying the type of rot will help you decide what further measures may be necessary. For example, when dry rot is in its death-throes it can still actively destroy timber. In these situations, measures to isolate the rot from the timber may need to be taken. Wet rots come in all shapes, sizes and colours. Like dry rot they die back once their water source has been cut off. In all cases, what you do about the wood that has been damaged by decay depends on its function. If rots have attacked structural timbers such as roof timbers or timber lintels then physical repairs may be required. In other situations, a superficial repair may suffice. The over-riding principle is to ensure that the minimum of original timber is removed. The problem is that people within the timber-treatment industry have differing ideas as to what this means.

The culture of removing timber within a metre of the last known area of an outbreak of dry rot has been an industry standard for decades. Enormous amounts of damage have been done in the past to buildings where the metre rule has been applied stringently. There are different schools of thought now that take a much more environmentally friendly approach to dealing with decay, which avoid the use of chemicals, and also conserve much more of the building fabric than previous methods.

Remember that it is usually in the interests of timber treatment companies to recommend some form of treatment work. Some companies may not be familiar with current thinking on treatment or may not feel inclined to agree with a softer approach. If you are concerned about the possible structural consequences of a severely affected timber then consult an engineer, architect or surveyor knowledgeable in old buildings.

One final word of warning, rots are fungi and if the moisture is allowed to come back at any time in the future, then you can have a new outbreak of rot. The spores are virtually everywhere in the atmosphere, you will never extinguish those, so all they need is some water to help them re-establish.

Left – The external walls of this house had been covered with cement render and plastic masonry paint, the internal walls were painted with textured impermeable paint. Water entered the fabric through cracks in the external render. The house was shut up for long periods of time with no ventilation. Dry rot became well established in this door frame.

Below – Cracks in the cement render allowed water to get into the wall which could not dry out again because of the impervious nature of the render and the masonry paint covering. In time the water rotted the timber window lintel.

5

Maintenance, repair and what to avoid

As discussed in the previous chapter, it is imperative that water does not get into the building. Similarly, the drains must not leak and the surface of the paint finish on timberwork has to be continuous to prevent water ingression.

How to approach maintenance and repairs of particular elements

Other areas of repairs and maintenance that do not play such a vital part in keeping moisture out of the fabric of the house may have a more relaxed attitude taken towards them.

If a number of bricks or stones have damaged faces, providing the cause of this decay has been halted, it is usually aesthetically more appropriate to leave the decayed bricks or stones as they are, so that the overall visual appeal of a wall is not scarred, although brick and stone can be replaced or invisibly repaired.

One of the joys of living in an old house is that you are surrounded by the patina of age on the materials used, so enjoy these for what they are rather than trying to make them look artificially new. The best compliment that can be made about a repair to an old house is that it is unnoticeable.

Whenever you are going to carry out maintenance and repairs to an old house ask yourself the following:

- Is this work necessary? Is there really a fault or am I expecting too much or looking for excuses to make a change?
- How much original fabric will be destroyed during this repair?
- Can using an alternative solution reduce the amount of original fabric destroyed?

By answering these questions you are likely to arrive at the minimum amount of work required to keep an old house sensitively maintained.

Inappropriate repairs

The use of inappropriate or incompatible materials on an old building is more difficult to deal with. This is because the damage has already been set in motion.

While it may be desirable to replace the offending material, this may not always be practicable. For example, where a hard replacement sand and cement mortar has started to damage old brick or stonework it is virtually impossible to remove without causing further physical damage to the surrounding bricks or stones.

Imagine that you are able to travel back in time to the date when your house was first built. What materials would have been available then? Timber, bricks, stone and earth, with lime and earth mortars to hold them together and limewashes to cover the walls both internally and externally. These are the materials with which to repair and maintain the building. They are compatible with the way in which the house was built and are widely available once more.

Conversely, the vast majority of materials developed and used in the latter half of the twentieth century are not very compatible with old buildings. Modern finishes and fittings tend to block dampness and require a rigid structure. Replacement all-metal or plastic doors and windows are less adaptable than timber to the movement that occurs in old houses as a result of seasonal variations.

It is rare that an old house has not had some inappropriate things done to it in the past. Due to twentieth-century alterations many old houses are now hybrids of tradition and modern building construction. The way they originally performed has been compromised and it can be difficult to assess how the two regimes are interacting. It makes sense to revert to the traditional where this is feasible since the building can never be totally modern.

The costs involved in un-picking past work can be high, so if you are considering buying an old house be aware of the problems you could be taking on. Make sure you get an idea of the costs to put things right (assuming this is desirable or possible) before purchasing the house.

Where changes to the fabric of a listed building are proposed, even if they are a reversal of previously inappropriate actions such as replacing

PVCu windows with timber (PVCu means unplasticised PVC), listed building consent would usually be required as this is an alteration.

Rainwater and drainage disposal

This is possibly the most important consideration in looking after old houses. If this is not working properly there is a huge potential for water to get into the fabric of the house and start decay.

Leaves and debris should be removed from gutters, downpipes and gulleys in the spring and after the leaves have fallen in the autumn. Cast iron guttering and downpipes often survive on old houses and are very durable provided they are maintained and regularly painted, paying special attention to the backs adjacent to walls. Where the paint finish is damaged or missing, water can seep under the paint finish and, unable to escape, causes rust to start. Where the downpipe brackets are offset from the walls on mounting blocks, this allows the rear face of the pipes to be painted more easily. If not the pipes must be removed for effective painting.

Long term, downpipes can rust right through and start discharging water onto the wall. Replacement rainwater sections where necessary, should be in cast iron to match the original pattern. Old patterns, with fixing ears are still available, and in imperial sizes.

If the downpipes do not drain into the public sewers around the house, they may drain into soakaways. These are underground rubble-filled pits that are required under current building regulations to be located at least five metres away from the building. In the past and before compliance with building regulations was necessary, these soakaways could often be much closer to old houses and rather small, which resulted in water running back under the house rather than being taken away from it.

Investigate exactly where the drains and soakaways are located and whether they are functioning correctly.

If new drain runs do have to be dug be aware that around old houses archaeological material could be dug up during excavations. Such work may be subject to listed building approval for listed houses, and building regulations approval for all dwellings.

Plastic gutters and downpipes have often been used as a cheap replacement for cast iron, however such changes to the character of an old house can detract from its overall appearance. Plastic gutters can expand and contract many more times than cast iron, so that movement at the joints may cause leaks to start. They are also much more likely to sag between brackets over time which may hamper water draining away easily and the plastic is prone to degrade in sunlight.

While cast iron is more expensive, providing it is properly and regularly painted to keep rust to a minimum, it can last much longer than PVC and is therefore argued to be more environmentally friendly.

Where a house is listed, listed building consent is usually required to change between cast iron and plastic rainwater or soil pipes.

Left – Cast iron gutters look more appropriate on old houses than plastic guttering and may even have decorative features like this lion's head at the junction between two sections.

Cast iron downpipes will last a very long time providing they are painted so that rust does not get established – especially at the backs of the downpipes.

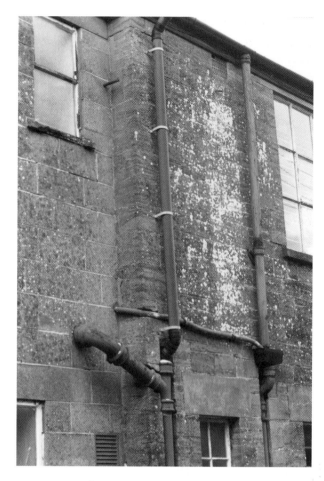

Think carefully about the visual impact of new soil stacks on the overall appearance of an elevation.

Roof leaks

Establishing the cause of the leak can be the most difficult part of the problem (see illustration on page 46).

If it concerns slipped or missing roof tiles or slates, these can generally be re-fixed in position, or renewed if damaged. However, care must be taken when working on roofs to avoid damaging further slates or tiles.

There will come a time where more than a few tiles or slates have slipped, due to the fixings generally beginning to rust, or the battens decaying. At this time it may be more cost-effective to have the roof re-laid, salvaging the sound roof tiles or slates and re-laying the roof and perhaps taking advantage of a breathable textile underlay.

New tiles or slates that are necessary to complete the roof could be located in areas where they are either invisible from the ground or randomly mixed in with the existing.

Junctions in roofs are likely problem areas. The mortar between ridge or hip tiles may be missing and lead flashings cracked, allowing water into the roof space. Mortar pointing around ridge tiles and chimney flaunchings is by definition very exposed. Eventually, over the passage of decades, the mortar will wear away or crack. (Builders are tempted to use cement mortars for repairs here but hydraulic lime mortars may be suitable in these locations – see Appendix.)

Valley gutters are renowned for leaking unless very carefully detailed and maintained. The back gutter behind a chimney can also be a weak point. Both these types of gutters are usually out of sight and easily forgotten in the twice yearly clear out.

The top layers of a thatch roof gradually decay over the years. Running repairs are possible but when it is coming to the end of its life problems can start to occur.

Old built-up roofing felt on flat-roofed extensions is also likely to become troublesome. Pay particular attention to where these materials adjoin other types of finishes. Asphalt has a better record than the cheaper three-layer felt but they all tend to have a relatively short lifespan compared with pitched roofs and need to be carefully checked for signs of developing leaks.

Generally flat roofs do not look appropriate on extensions to old buildings (there is little historical precedent as in the past a flat roof was only possible with metal since lead was too expensive for most buildings), so when replacement is necessary see if a roof pitched at an angle which matches the rest of the house is reasonable. Often it will not be possible to fit but some degree of improvement might be available. Remember that each traditional roof covering has a minimum angle at which it works best, and this determines the shape of houses in the locality. Slate (in certain sizes) and pantiles can be laid at relatively shallow angles in sheltered locations, whereas thatch and plain tiles need to be set more steeply.

When looking for the source of a roof leak, don't expect to find a large hole, it can be surprisingly small yet still be able to admit large quantities of water. Where roofs have been leaking for some time before action is taken, some of the roof timbers may have started to rot. These need to be allowed to dry out if still damp, and careful repairs carried out to ensure that the maximum amount of the original fabric is kept braced or splinted, if necessary by new timbers.

Seasonal changes have their effects on roofs. Lead is well known for its ability to expand in the heat but, if it is too restricted, it will buckle and eventually crack and allow water to get into a building. Lead needs to be broken up into short lengths to cope with thermal expansion and carefully detailed to work properly.

Roofing materials – stone slates, slates and clay roofing tiles

These are usually recyclable depending on conditions. Stone slates, slates and clay roofing tiles can all be carefully taken off an existing roof ready for re-use. The damaged stone slates or slates can often be re-sized. New stone slates or slates may be used in areas where they are not particularly visible, so that over time they will weather down.

New clay roofing tiles will need to be supplied where any of these are damaged or cracked, but again these can be used in less visible places while they weather down.

The right-hand roof has been replaced with concrete tiles which seem to have made for an awkward junction that needs extra covering.

Old peg tiles have variations in size and colour not available in modern machine-made tiles.

Replacement artificial slates and concrete roof tiles

Replacing the whole roof covering with artificial slates or concrete roof tiles is, rightly or wrongly, perceived by some as being cheaper than re-using and re-fixing the existing roof covering. This is not appropriate to an old house. Artificial slates and tiles can look false on old houses as they do not equate to their natural counterparts in texture, colour or variety.

Where overall lifecycle costs are considered, including the environmental cost of producing manufactured materials, natural materials like slate are often claimed to come out better.

A change in roof covering can mean a change in weight on the roof timbers. Where one roof is replaced in a terrace of houses the junctions between the existing and the new roofing material is likely to be a weak point where water could enter.

Even modern handmade clay roofing tiles are subject to the same, almost unavoidable compromises that also affect modern bricks. The traditionally used, local superficial clay deposits are mostly worked-out and so clay is now taken from deeper deposits in fewer locations. The colours of modern clay tiles are sometimes produced by applied minerals rather than being a natural expression of fired local clay. Be aware that when matching new clay tiles with old that the old clay tiles were once bright red, yellow, white or orange and may have weathered to a dark, almost purple colour in some cases. Modern versions may not weather in exactly the same way. Try to find examples of weathered new tiles to see how they look after a few years.

For listed buildings, listed building consent would be required for completely changing the roofing material and consent would not usually be granted. In conservation areas planning permission can be required for a change in the material used to cover the roof.

Originally all clay tiled like the centre roof. The right hand roof has been replaced with concrete tiles and the left covered with a remedial material (if this cannot be removed from the tiles they cannot be salvaged for re-use).

Comparison between stone and slate roofs. This shows the potential difficulty of making a satisfactory junction.

Remedial materials to keep old roof tiles in place

A number of proprietary products are sold to be applied as waterproofing to the top of the existing roof covering, and foam-glue sprays that can be applied to the underside of existing roofs. These treatments are sold as remedial measures and to stop slates and tiles from slipping when the nail fixings begin to rust through. When tiles or slates are permanently adhered with both types of product, it means they are less re-useable.

These products are short-term solutions and the subsequent re-roofing costs can be much higher if none of the original roof covering can be re-used. There are also concerns that these materials seal-up the natural ventilation between tiles and, in the case of the underside treatments, concerns that encasing old untreated timber battens and rafter edges reduces their exposure to ventilating air and could thereby provide conditions for decay to take hold.

Replacement of straw thatch with water reed

There are three principal types of thatching material: combed wheat reed, long straw thatch and water reed. There are regional variations in all parts of the country of thatching materials and thatching styles, which include heather, seaweed and bracken in Scotland.

This long straw thatched roof has a raised 'block' ridge, as used with water reed, and stitches at the eaves ('liggers') as used with long straw thatch.

Changing from either of the straw types to water reed can involve the removal of all existing thatch. It has traditionally been the custom to leave the lower layers of existing thatch in place, so that these original layers may date back many hundreds of years, depending on the age of the house. These lower layers may contain valuable archaeology, including evidence of mediaeval smoke blackening to the underside of the thatch if it has existed that long. It would be regrettable to lose this.

The woven wattle frame supporting the underside of the thatch is smoke blackened, indicating that this is mediaeval thatch (an open fire would have caused the blackening). Care needs to be taken when re-thatching to avoid the loss of this archaeological evidence.

A bundle of Norfolk water reed as used for thatching.

Where a house is listed, listed building consent may be required for changing the thatching material or the details used, so speak to the local conservation officer first.

The thickness of the thatch keeps out the water. Where wire netting has been placed over new thatch over a period a gap grows between the netting and the thatch signalling the time is near for repair. Carrying out running repairs should extend the life of the thatch.

Television aerials and satellite dishes

Choose discreet locations for these away from the principal elevations. Television aerials can be hidden behind chimneys or, if reception allows, in roof spaces so that they do not spoil the look of the house. An aerial amplifier can boost roof space aerials. The arrival of digital terrestrial television could potentially provide better tolerance of poor signals, so aerial location may be even less critical.

Think carefully about siting television aerials on old houses, apart from the visual considerations, fixing and stability need careful thought.

Satellite dishes can sometimes function well hidden in roof valleys or even in a remote location in the garden. Installers will usually want to site aerials and dishes in the easiest location for wiring and reception, which may not be the best place visually, so think what is most appropriate for the house rather than the installer's convenience. Make sure that cable-runs across the house do not damage the fabric or appearance.

Where satellite dishes are to be installed on listed buildings, or in certain locations on houses in conservation areas, local authority consents are required. A booklet called *A Householder's Planning Guide for the Installation of Satellite Television Dishes* is available from the government (ODPM) website.

Roof ventilation

This is necessary to help avoid insect and fungal attack of timbers and is often inadvertently reduced in several ways by laying impermeable roofing felt or sealing up gaps in roof spaces with insulation, without ensuring that sufficient ventilation space is maintained to keep the roof timbers aired.

Before underlays were used roofs had lots of air passing through them around the tiles or slates, thus keeping the roof timbers well-ventilated and allowing moisture that got into roof spaces to dry out again. Impervious roofing felts, or underlays, around since the 1950s, were laid over the existing roof timbers and fixed in position under tiling battens when re-roofing was being carried out. Where these roofing felts have been added it was not initially perceived as necessary to ventilate the existing roof space, until subsequent dampness in roof timbers was identified and attributed to a lack of ventilation. By that time some twenty or thirty years of experience had shown what damage could be caused.

The introduction of roof insulation between rafters has a similar effect, because this stops air circulating around the timbers and any dampness that gets into the timbers is less likely to be able to escape. When insulation gets wet as a result of a roof leak, for example, it is difficult to dry out *in situ*, and if not lifted can cause rots to start attacking the roof timbers or the timber plaster-laths it touches. It can also lose its insulating properties until it has dried out again.

These problems can be combated to a certain extent by the introduction of greater amounts of natural ventilation at eaves and ridge levels, as now required under the building regulations, when roofs are re-laid.

These twentieth-century buildings being demolished show old impervious felt underlay on the left, and water reed used under the tiles of the right-hand roof.

Vapour-permeable roofing underlays have been widely available since the middle of the 1990s. These shed water getting through the slates and tiles, like older underlays do, but also should allow a certain amount of air to pass through, depending on type, in order to ventilate the roof-space without installing additional ventilators. Evaluation of the effectiveness of this new technology in old houses may take a few years.

Timber doors, windows and decorative timber features

The original windows and doors are usually the most important architectural features of any old house, so it is vitally important that these are sympathetically repaired and retained. They are part of the original fabric and face of an old house. Old doors and windows are usually repairable and it is comparatively rare that complete replacement is necessary. Statutory consents may be necessary for such changes.

Modern replacement timber windows made between the 1950s and 1970s, when the quality of softwood joinery timber generally used was not particularly high, are far more likely to rot than earlier windows. Those mid-twentieth-century windows are not necessarily indicative of the performance of either ancient or modern timber windows. More recent windows hope to have addressed these problems.

When approaching the repair of old timber windows, the absolute minimum of original timber should be removed to enable repairs to be carried out. Small areas of decay can be filled with putty or fillers according to circumstance, while larger areas of decay may need to have new timber carefully spliced in to form a repair. Where loose joints are evident the wedges can usually be replaced, but if reinforcement is appropriate, angled non-corroding concealed metal brackets may be appropriate to let into the wood.

When carrying out repairs to old windows always make sure the old glass is carefully looked after as it can easily be scratched when the paint on the frame is being sanded down or broken during removal of damaged old putty. Wet abrading with wire wool is a kinder alternative for preparing narrow glazing bars (and helps avoid raising dust).

Some windows may not be operable because they have been painted up in the past and freeing them now will take time and effort. It may not be necessary to always have every sash operable if doing so risks damage and there are others working.

Repairs to old doors and any decorative features such as bargeboards, follow the same principles of repair as for old windows in that

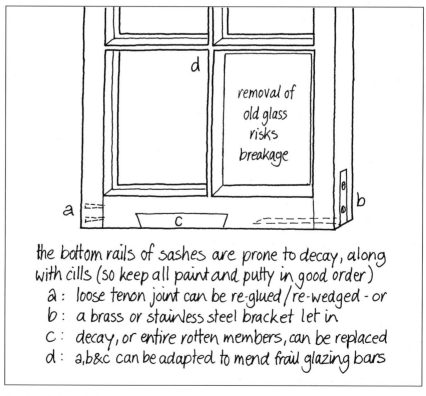

the bottom rails of sashes are prone to decay, along with cills (so keep all paint and putty in good order)
a : loose tenon joint can be re-glued/re-wedged - or
b : a brass or stainless steel bracket let in
c : decay, or entire rotten members, can be replaced
d : a,b&c can be adapted to mend frail glazing bars

Repair of timber windows.

Georgian sash windows had glazing bars as shown in the windows on the second floor of this house. The Victorians produced glass in larger sheets so glazing bars became unnecessary.

the maximum of original fabric is to be kept and the minimum removed when repairs are necessary.

When all these elements have been carefully repaired, they must be thoroughly painted afterwards (ideally with a vapour-permeable or breathable traditional finish) to ensure that the paint surface remains intact to avoid decay becoming established.

A contributory factor in the decay of joinery timber is the quality of the paint. Traditional and some modern, vapour-permeable paints are better at keeping the wood dry during the life of the coating, whereas the types of paint that are prone to crack and peel (again most popular in the mid-twentieth century) will admit water which cannot easily escape.

Where dog and cat flaps need to be inserted in doors consider their location carefully so that they are reversible when no longer required. Where a modern door or wall exists try to use these instead of older parts of the house. Listed building consent may be necessary where the house is listed.

A cared-for 'Yorkshire' sliding sash window, these slide horizontally rather than vertically so that weights and pulleys are not required.

Metal windows

Iron casement windows are susceptible to rust where the paint finish has failed.

Usually when the rust is removed there may be sufficient sound metal underneath, so that further repairs are not needed, but these can be sensitively carried out where necessary.

The most important part of decorating old metal windows is to ensure that all rust is removed and quality metal primers applied to protect the surfaces, before being carefully and thoroughly painted so that rust does not become established again.

Where leaded lights are incorporated into metal casements, the lead cames used to join the individual pieces of glass together can be renewed or re-sealed, where defective, while retaining the old glass.

Secondary glazing and draught-proofing

Secondary glazing and draught-proofing can be sensitively added to old windows so that they are not irreversibly damaged – if carefully thought through beforehand to avoid any of the old fabric having to be cut away to accommodate them. However, this has to be balanced against the need for old houses to have a minimum background level of ventilation for them to breathe and avoid the build up of condensation and decay. There is little point sealing up every crack around the windows if you then need to add some other form of permanent ventilation.

The current building regulations even make provision for new windows to have trickle vents designed into them, which allow for air circulation without compromising the security of the window. The government guidance on listed buildings, currently PPG 15, does allow for these regulations to be applied flexibly where listed buildings are concerned and where double glazing or trickle vents would look out of place.

Part L1 of the 2001 building regulations – Conservation of Fuel and Power in Dwellings – makes specific reference to the need to conserve the special character of historic buildings, which in this context includes listed buildings and buildings in a conservation area.

Interestingly, the amount of ventilation a trickle vent provides is probably equivalent to that which gets in around an old sash window, the difference being that a trickle vent can be closed.

Replacement windows and doors

The types of replacement windows and doors that are least likely to be appropriate to old houses are aluminium, PVCu and standard factory-made modern wooden windows and doors. All references to windows in this section could equally apply to doors.

Aluminium windows were popular before PVCu windows became available. Both types are made from a less accommodating material than the original timber windows they replaced. They can distort if there is any slight structural movement. Adjusting metal and plastic windows to open once movement has occurred is not always possible and is less straightforward than easing a timber window.

The idea that PVCu windows are maintenance free is now being questioned (there are now paint finishes available for them) and their anticipated life span is currently expected by some to compare less favourably than initially anticipated, with replacement becoming necessary after 20 to 25 years. There are growing concerns about the effects of the manufacture of PVC on the environment and how this material is disposed of when replacement is necessary.

Standard factory made timber windows have often been fitted into existing houses by making the existing opening larger to fit the window rather than adjusting the window. This often means that they are not very sympathetic to the existing proportions of an old house, as well as being of inappropriate design and detail.

Timber used for joinery during the Edwardian period and earlier was allowed to season naturally and consequently lasted much longer, and the timbers used were also of a more durable species or part of the tree. The type of fast grown kiln-dried joinery timber used during the 1960s and 1970s has tended to rot quicker.

Replacing inappropriate windows in old houses is usually possible, using purpose made joinery of an appropriate design to the existing house. These can enhance the overall appearance of the house and, as the earlier problems of timber seasoning have been understood and preservative treatments are widely used, the new windows should last longer.

If the size of the window openings was increased when replacement windows were fitted then this presents another problem. Reducing the size of window openings to be more in keeping with the rest of the general appearance of the house is possible but finding matching bricks or stones to make the openings smaller may be a challenge.

An alternative is to have new purpose made joinery designed to suit the existing size of openings. The problem here is that large window openings can often look out of character in an old house, where windows were traditionally a less prominent feature in the overall design.

Where a house is listed, an application for listed building consent would be necessary for modern replacement windows. Where the original windows still exist permission is unlikely to be granted. In some conservation areas a planning application would be required, and probably refused.

Replacement glass

Do not replace old glass if at all possible as it can be of historic importance in itself. Its modern replacement is float glass that came into use in the middle of the twentieth century, made by floating molten glass across the surface of molten tin. The thickness of the glass is consistent and the surfaces are very flat creating an almost optically perfect glass.

You can usually tell what type of glass you are looking through by moving your head from side to side. If you don't see any distortion in the glass, then it is more likely to be a modern glass. The qualities of glass produced by earlier methods such as crown and cylinder glass are very different to modern day glass.

When replacing broken glass (in locations that do not need to comply with the building regulations for safety glass) it is sensible to use new handmade glass that complements the existing. The imperfections in handmade glass should be subtle. Avoid over-worked modern versions that are too rich in bubbles and ridges.

Existing old glass can be protected to an extent by applying a safety film. Take care if you remove this as the surface of old glass is susceptible to scratching. New handmade glass can also be supplied specially converted to safety glass.

Sunlight through Georgian hand-made glass highlights the subtle imperfections.

Three different types of patterned glass on one internal door.

(Re-pointing brickwork and stonework)

There will come a time when re-pointing is necessary, but it is unlikely that all the mortar will fail at the same time, as this process usually happens over a number of years or decades. Therefore, when re-pointing is carried out it will be piecemeal in small areas rather than whole sections of wall being re-pointed at the same time.

It is a mistake to think that re-pointing with a strong, hard cement mortar will last forever. Experience shows that it is capable of accelerating the decay of old bricks or stones. If the original pointing was a lime and sand mortar then that is what is usually appropriate to use when re-pointing.

The art of re-pointing is that when it is complete, it should be stylistically identical to the original pointing – assuming that this has itself been carefully carried out. The only clue that a wall has areas of re-pointing should usually be that there is lighter coloured mortar, until it

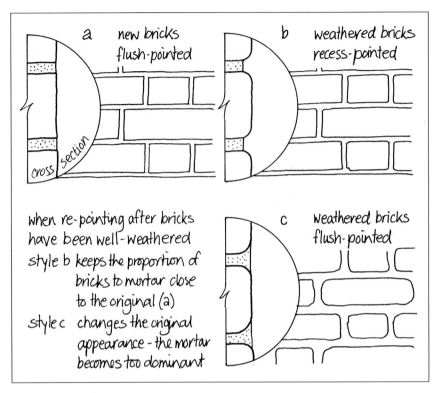

a   new bricks
flush-pointed

b   weathered bricks
recess-pointed

cross section

when re-pointing after bricks
have been well-weathered
style b keeps the proportion of
bricks to mortar close
to the original (a)
style c changes the original
appearance - the mortar
becomes too dominant

c   weathered bricks
flush-pointed

Plain re-pointing of brickwork.

has weathered down after a few years. Good pointing and re-pointing is about making sure that the new mortar is flush with, or very slightly recessed from the face of the bricks or stones. Where the edges of the masonry are slightly ragged a recessed finish is often best.

Once the lime mortar has begun to set a textured finish can be achieved, if desired, by using a brush to stipple the finish. The skill is to know when to tend the finish. Re-pointing using lime is an exacting skill as any mortar that does get onto the face of the bricks or stones by mistake will usually leave a whitish mark.

A cement-based mortar is not best matched to soft old bricks or stonework. It can inhibit free movement of moisture out of the wall leading to premature decay. Where a wall has already been re-pointed using a cement-based mortar, it might just be possible to remove it. Often the film of cement was poorly applied and you may be able to pick a thin skin of cement off the underlying lime if you are lucky. If the cement was applied thoroughly (re-pointing should be at least 25 mm deep), or if it is covering the faces of the bricks then you have a more serious problem – removal of the cement might easily also remove the faces of the bricks or stones, so there is little that can be done. ⟩ *Recommendation*

Never be tempted to allow the use of power tools when removing pointing. Disc-cutters may be fine in theory for this task but they can widen joints and leave behind hundreds of accidental disfiguring grooves in the bricks or stones that can never be undone. However in certain circumstances some careful drilling, using a drill bit with a diameter that is less than the width of the joints, may reduce the amount of potentially damaging impact from hammers and chisels, though drilling should not be allowed to disfigure faces of bricks that might later be taken out and re-used.

Where old lime-based mortar has decayed to a stage where it needs to be raked out and replaced, the replacement mortar mix and the style of pointing used need to match the original as closely as possible. This is because the appearance of a wall can be quite dramatically altered if the balance between the amount of stone or brick visible and the apparent width or style of the surrounding mortar joints is changed. No competent craftsperson would ever be proud of mortar smeared over the edges of bricks or stones. Re-pointing finished with a weather-struck (angled) edge or standing proud is not appropriate to the character of old houses and are styles associated with cement.

Cement re-pointing (intended as a repair) has trapped water in these bricks which are decaying as a result.

Special historic pointing finishes, such as penny and tuck pointing may have been replaced by conventional pointing in the recent past but the skills to replace tuck pointing still exist and seamless repairs are possible by modern craftspeople using lime mixes.

When this wall was re-pointed the old mortar was not removed to a sufficient depth so the new pointing, which was cement and incompatible with the lime behind, has fallen out.

Cement 'ribbon' pointing on this stonework draws the eye to the pointing rather than the stonework, this would not have been the original intention.

Above – Dark cement pointing on this chalk wall detracts from the character, it could also damage the chalk.

A different section of the same chalk wall that has not been re-pointed.

Pointing can change the character of walls, sometimes it will weather back to match but that will depend on the mix and whether the amount of visible mortar has been increased.

Two types of pointing to pebbles – the lower panel has 'struck' pointing which competes with the pebbles, while the upper panel shows the pebbles off.

Pointing starting to weather on the left side of the picture. New ribbon pointing on the right changes the character of this stone wall.

Brick quoins contrast with flint – until they are painted. Meter boxes can be a problem so seek all options with the supplier.

Flint and pebble walls

When a flint or pebble wall was originally constructed, great care was taken to select flints or pebbles that matched and complemented each other on a wall surface. The same care should be taken when repairs are being carried out. If stones have been lost add matching ones rather that thinning out the existing ones, so that the rhythm of the wall is maintained.

Unskilled pointing can damage the visual appeal of an existing flint or pebble wall, where the mortar is allowed to smother or obscure the original walling material.

On a well-pointed flint wall the mortar should not be the dominant element and should match existing pointing providing that it, too, was sensitively carried out. Care should be taken to avoid patches of re-pointing standing out in a different style as this detracts from the visual appeal of the wall.

Repairing brickwork

Where old bricks have decayed to such an extent that they cannot be reused by turning them around (which can be done to the occasional brick if the wall is set in lime mortar), then replacement bricks should be selected that match as closely as possible in size, porosity, colour and texture to the existing. Select the new mortar to match the existing original historic mortar as closely as possible.

Finding modern bricks to match is time consuming. Mass-produced bricks are usually made from clay that is deep-mined and fired in large kilns, whereas older bricks were made from less compacted clay found closer to the surface and which had been naturally weathered before being dug. They were dried in the open air and fired in relatively small batches. This may mean that new bricks are harder and more uniform in appearance which can create an imbalance (especially if set in cement mortar) as moisture will not be able to evaporate at the same rate from all the bricks in the wall.

If the house is in a traditional brick area, it may be possible to find a small working brickworks that produces a good match for the quality and colour of old local bricks.

Replacing individual bricks requires similar care to re-pointing to ensure a careful match.

Repairing stonework

Where possible re-use any existing stones as trying to find new stones to match can be very difficult because the exact quarry may no longer exist and, even if it does, the new stone could come from different strata or another part of the quarry, so it may have different qualities.

Where stones have pieces missing, it is possible to use a mixture of stone dust, sands and lime to create a repair that can be carefully blended-in with the existing stonework by skilled craftspeople. This is

New stone repairs stand out on an otherwise weathered stone house. It is always difficult to know whether to blend with the original face or the weathered surface.

sometimes known as a plastic repair – though it has nothing to do with modern plastic. However, where this work is inexpertly carried out, water can in time get in between the existing stone and the repair causing further problems.

If stones have cracked, make sure that the cause of the cracking has been identified before repairs are carried out, otherwise the problem is likely to recur. Smooth-faced stonework cut into blocks, known as ashlar, may be held in position by iron cramps. Water may cause these cramps to rust over time, which then expand and crack the stone it was meant to restrain.

The visual appearance of any replacement stone (where replacement is absolutely necessary) and re-pointing should match the existing as closely as possible. In time the repairs tone down and they should hardly be noticeable against the existing stones.

Surface decay does not always warrant complete replacement but either way there is no point dealing with it until the cause has been dealt with.

Repairing renders and plasters

Where holes are to be repaired, make sure that the backing is sound and, on timber-framed walls, that any timber laths are securely fixed, otherwise the render finish will crack again.

The thickness of new plasters should match the old and if hair has been found in the surrounding plaster then this can be added to the same layers of the new so that it matches the existing as much as possible in function as well as appearance. As with all existing materials and mixes it is possible to have these analysed to establish what proportions were originally used, but an experienced craftsperson should be able to assess this.

External render is applied over timber laths on timber-framed houses. It is sometimes possible to re-use laths if they and their fixings are sound.

Making render and plaster repairs blend in with the existing is really down to the skill and eye of the person carrying out the work. Roughcast, which became known as pebbledash in the twentieth century, is where tiny stones are added to a slurry topcoat and thrown at the wall. Re-creating a finish that is similar to the original when matching-in, requires skill, practice and usually several sample areas to achieve the correct style.

Removing cement-based renders from walls may not be possible because it is so firmly adhered to the adjoining surfaces that removal will damage the original fabric. Every situation will be different and has to be assessed on its own merits as to whether it is practicable and possible to reverse or not.

If you find you are stuck with cement render you will have to carefully maintain it and fill any slight cracks to keep water out. If the cement render was applied over old lime render the situation is potentially worse as eventually the lime could be affected by trapped damp and shed its cement skin. One day re-rendering will be necessary. The unanswerable question, unless it is already hanging off, is when, and how much, damage is being done in the meantime to the wall beneath.

Cracks in a cement-based render are visible having been filled prior to re-decoration.

Earth walled buildings

Earth walled buildings are found in various parts of Scotland, around the Solway Firth, Wales, Lincolnshire, the East Midlands, East Anglia, Wessex and the West Country. This method of building is given different names in different parts of the country, often associated with the type of construction.

Cob is the name most commonly associated with earth walled buildings, usually found in the West Country. The walls of cob buildings are constructed using earth that has been mixed with straw, which is then compacted on top of the wall – usually by treading – in successive layers. Depending on the type of building, the completed wall was usually coated with a lime or earth-based render.

In East Anglia earth walled buildings are known as clay lump, as the walls were made from pre-fabricated moulded blocks of local boulder-clay. These were reinforced with straw or grass and once dried were laid in courses, like bricks, and coated with a clay slurry or earth-based render.

Keeping the earth walling dry is most important, so that it does not begin to disintegrate. Make sure that dampness is kept away from the base of the stone or brick plinth that the earth or cob walling is usually sitting on. Check that earth is not banked up against this plinth and that water drains away from the building rather than into it. Also, ensure that the roof covering has a sufficient overhang to protect the wall from water running down it. Gutters and downpipes, where they exist should be sufficient to take away the water from the building.

Earth walled buildings should only be repaired with similar materials, so cement mortars, renders and insulating blocks should be avoided as they expand and contract in a different way to the original materials and have different permeability. The completed wall surfaces of earth walled buildings were often limewashed, depending on their locality. Avoid using modern impervious paints that do not allow the earth walls to breathe.

Where cement renders have been applied over an earth wall this creates problems because when the wall moves very slightly through thermal expansion, the render detaches or cracks rather than moving with the wall, and these cracks allow water into the fabric of the building. Once the water is trapped behind the cement it can dissolve the earth wall behind. If cement render is already in place it is important to keep the surface free of cracks, alternatively, seek professional advice about removal of the cement (if this is feasible) and replacement with a traditional breathable lime or earth render.

There is renewed interest in earth walled buildings and some new buildings are being constructed based on these old methods.

Render and later alterations may be concealing an earth walled building beneath.

In this case a clay lump building built from blocks of dried clay-rich earth bound with straw.

Left – This earth walled building needs protection to stop it deteriorating further. It has lost its overhanging roof and rain is dissolving the wall. It needs a sympathetic breathable covering (cement would make things worse in the long run).

Below – A well cared for earth walled building with a good overhanging thatch roof and protective limewash.

Wattle and daub

This it the term used for the infill panels between the timbers in a timber-framed building, both internally and externally. Wattle is timber sticks woven or tied with twine into a support grid between timber framing. Daub is a mix of the locally available materials, such as earth, lime and sometimes animal dung which may have been reinforced with straw. This is applied in layers to the wattle framework to create a reasonably smooth surface finish between the timbers.

Any repairs to these panels should be carried out re-using similar materials to the original. Avoid using cement in any repair daub mix. The surface should be covered with limewash or internally with distemper, which allow the panels to breathe.

Timber weatherboarding

Old timber weatherboarding can become rather brittle and the nails used to hold the boards in place are usually embedded in the boards, so it is best to avoid disturbing them wherever possible. Ideally, where repairs are necessary due to decay, only the rotten areas should be replaced with the minimum of disturbance to the surrounding boards. Use a similar timber to the original for the repairs, since thin softwood will often curl when used in traditional board widths.

A variety of old weatherboarding.

Applying a decorative finish may be appropriate to match in with the existing boards, depending on the local vernacular. Some old black pitch or tar finishes may react with modern alternatives so check for compatibility first. Where weatherboarding is decorated with modern plastic paint, it may be possible to remove this to allow the timber to breathe again. Apply new vapour-permeable paints or traditional limewashes instead.

Narrow weatherboarding can be an indication of more recent machined timber.

Carefully painted ironwork can last for centuries.

Ironmongery and metalwork

Any ironwork features attached to the house can be carefully inspected for signs of rust and repainted on a regular basis in order to halt decay. Where features have been damaged or have rusted, it is usually possible to get them carefully repaired, if the right person is found. Pay particular attention to where ironwork is fixed to other materials and rarely painted, as this is a vulnerable point for rust to establish.

Paints

Breathable paints are the most appropriate to use on old buildings and these are often known as microporous. Availability of these paints is increasing and reading the small print on the back of the paint tin will usually give you an indication of whether a paint is breathable and/or flexible (though not usually by how much – and that is important). These are now available for use on external joinery and some interior surfaces.

A great many interior paints are not vapour permeable, so it is important to choose the type of paint before choosing the colour. If forced to use emulsion paint rather than traditional distemper or lime-wash then consider a low-vinyl emulsion (the type used by modern house-builders to first-coat walls while they are still drying out). Many paints are breathable to some extent but few are breathable to any useful extent on old buildings. You may need to seek impartial professional advice on this.

Many paints that are water-based will have plastic compounds, which do not allow the surface under the finished paint film to breathe. Paints that are water-based may not necessarly be breathable, though many breathable paints are water-based.

Be aware that processes like sizing a wall with paste before lining paper is applied will not allow it to breathe so well.

Lead was an ingredient in paint used on joinery until generally outlawed late in the twentieth century. The older formulations had a natural oil base and the metal component allowed them to weather into a powder rather than split or blister.

Traditional oil paints for use on timberwork are being re-introduced. These may have linseed oil as a base and other components instead of the traditional lead. If you have bare timber to paint, or perhaps previous lead paint intact, these paint systems can be a reasonable compromise provided they weather and breathe like lead paint.

Ideally each and every layer of a finish and background in an old house must be equally breathable, not just one or two layers. Traditionally the whole thickness of the construction of a wall was more or less uniformly vapour-permeable. The introduction of an impermeable layer can be damaging and set up a situation where water vapour is trapped in the construction.

Mixing the two regimes by using modern paints on traditional construction can be damaging and if you are unsure about what your house already has acquired then seek professional advice. Any paints that do not allow the fabric of an old house to breathe freely are best avoided as they will not allow any moisture that gets into the fabric to evaporate out quickly again, thus storing up decay problems for the future. Examples of these are modern-day gloss, masonry and most emulsion paints. All were used almost universally during the last half of the twentieth century.

Limewash and distempers on the other hand are breathable finishes, which allow moisture to evaporate out of the fabric (unless they are bound with oils).

For external walls, plastic-based masonry paints may have been applied to most old houses at some stage during their recent history. It is rare to find an old house that has avoided these types of paints. Removing plastic masonry paints from the bricks or renders of old buildings is beneficial to their ability to breathe again – any dampness that gets into the fabric of the house will then be able to get out again. A breathable finish like limewash can then be applied for additional protection, to maintain this permeability and to blend any repairs.

Where walls have been covered with cement renders it may be possible to reinstate these areas with lime render as limewash alone will not enable the house to breathe.

It is now usually possible to remove most types of modern paints from old houses. Each house and its problems are different, and each situation has to be assessed on its individual merits. It is always advisable to carry out samples first to see how effective the chosen method is likely to be.

The disadvantages of sand-blasting (an early paint removal technique), is that it can be very ferocious and remove the original fabric with the paint so its use is avoided. Where a building is listed, listed building consent is usually not granted for this more extreme treatment. However, recent developments in more sensitive techniques such as vortex systems, steam strippers and more environmentally friendly chemical paint-strippers mean that it may now be possible to carefully remove most types of impermeable paint without damaging the original fabric beneath, providing they are used sensitively.

A word of caution – masonry paint can sometimes mask relatively recent repairs in non-original materials so be prepared to address these, or cover them up again with the preferred limewash.

Depending on the types of paint, and how they have adhered to the substrate, the complete removal of the plastic paint may not be entirely possible without risking damage. If you have done as much paint removal as you can you may have to compromise and cover the whole area with new limewash and be prepared to experiment with ways of making it adhere to any remaining plastic paint or cement.

Adding tallow to limewash is a traditional way of increasing durability but this does limit its breathability.

It is beneficial to an old house to remove plastic masonry paint, although costly. Where the render has small pebbles on the surface (roughcast or pebbledash in England, harling in Scotland) and is painted, removing the paint totally may be almost impossible. However, you might remove enough to make limewashing worthwhile visually at least.

Where you have plastic paint on cement render there is really only a visual benefit to be gained from limewashing, if you can make it adhere. Usually old houses have acquired a mix of layers of lime render and cement render repairs with a top coat of plastic paint. Anyone lucky enough to have limewash on a lime rendered or brick or stone wall, however, merely applies another coat of limewash every few years and does not have to worry so much about hairline cracks, since the wall finish should not retain water long-term.

Proprietary long-life paints are often applied by firms or franchises with the implication that you may never need to decorate again. Even if that promise is borne out, the old house owner has to be alert to whether these finishes can accommodate movement or breathe to any really useful degree.

Scientifically, it is no doubt possible to show that everything breathes and is flexible at least to some extent. In fact, even plastic masonry paints breathe – just not enough to be worthwhile to most old buildings. Whatever the type of modern paint, once applied it is uniform and lacks the intrinsic colour and texture variations that make limewash so attractive.

Painting one house in a group can alter the balance of the composition.

Unpainted external walls

Where pebbledash or roughcast has never been painted, avoid doing so otherwise it will become a maintenance liability in the future and if impervious paint finishes are used these can lead to water getting trapped and causing future damp problems as already discussed.

It is sensible not to paint existing brick or stone walls for the same technical reasons, but if you must then use a traditional limewash. Painting any previously unpainted wall can significantly alter the character of an old house in a way that is usually aesthetically obvious and so would usually require listed building consent for a listed house.

Damp sealants

Damp sealants of various types, claim to stop water getting into walls. The problem is that water may enter not only from rain but also as condensation from inside, by rising up from the ground or soaking down from faulty roofs and cracks then may not be able to get out. In practice, this can mean storing up decay problems for the future. Damp sealants are sometimes used in desperation to stop a problem that may have an alternative solution that is kinder to the building, and which does not permanently alter the fabric. Professionals involved in the conservative care of historic buildings therefore rarely regard damp sealants as a first line of treatment.

Similar caution should be adopted with those damp-sealants and similar materials designed to hold water back from entering the house from damp walls. It is better to seek out and tackle the cause rather than dam-up the problem.

Injected damp-proof courses

Injected damp-proof courses have been an automatic response to damp walls for decades, often fostered by mortgage lenders' requirements. They have frequently been sold on the basis of a survey by the people who install them, rather than through an independent assessment, though many professionals still resort to this method.

If the principle of injecting chemicals into a wall to form a water barrier is sound in theory, it can come unstuck in practice with old properties. Old properties rely on generous pathways for water to dry out. Putting additional barriers in place can inhibit this. Even if the dpc stops damp in one place, any ground water under slight pressure will

Painting architectural details alters the appearance and can be very difficult to reverse. The door on the right has been replaced.

find somewhere else to escape. It is not the answer to damp-proof every-thing. It can be very effective to install a French drain, which is a way of providing somewhere for water to evaporate easily around the building, so that it will be less able to migrate up the walls (illustration page 48).

The ancillary work that many dpc installation companies have required customers to undertake to qualify for their guarantees will, in some cases, remove the prime causes of dampness alone – such as keep-ing earth away from walls, repairing drains and rainwater goods, and dealing with condensation. The often standard requirement for re-plas-tering can be unnecessarily destructive and introduces yet more mod-ern, perhaps incompatible, materials into an old house.

As discussed earlier, dampness in old buildings is often the result of a combination of causes. Ensure that the fabric of the house is able to breathe as universally as possible. Ensure that impervious materials have not been applied to, or laid immediately adjacent to, the external walls and that earth is not banked up against the walls. In addition, the problems created by people living in a house, like creating condensa-tion, may be combated by the use of appropriate ventilation, heating or even de-humidifiers.

When a solution to dampness has been instigated it can take many months or years for the fabric to dry out again and reach equilibrium. Dampness drying out can look identical to a continuing problem,

Injected damp-proof courses can disfigure walls.

especially if plasters and finishes have absorbed soluble salts, so time, patience and understanding are necessary.

Other forms of retrospectively fitted dpcs you may find in an old house are porous tubes drilled into the outside walls; a copper wire (sometimes with an electrical current applied) which was said to alter the polarity affecting water in the structure, or a physical waterproof barrier mechanically cut into the walls.

Damp-proof membranes (dpms) are a similar conventional solution for floors and may be found as a waterproof paint over a concrete sub-floor or a sheet of polythene. They should ideally be assessed as part of the general damp-management of an old house rather than being installed automatically, since they are potentially quite disruptive.

Timber treatment against insect and fungi

Installers issue timber treatment guarantees after quantities of chemicals have been pumped or sprayed into an old house in order to poison the insects and fungi that are living off damp timber, but the guarantee may only cover the treated area.

Ways of reducing dampness have been discussed earlier in the book. Take away the attractive damp environment and the insects and fungi should slowly diminish. Insecticides might kill the pest insects but they also kill any insect predators. Pests such as deathwatch beetle spend time deep inside wood and may re-use old flight holes so may escape the poison only to emerge to find all the spiders and insects that once wanted to eat them are dead (see Chapter 4).

Timber treatment regimes require chemicals to be either surface applied or pressure impregnated into affected timbers. Environmental and health considerations, chemical pollution, toxicity to wildlife and even to humans have been subjects for serious concern over this.

Bats can be harmed by chemical spays, so advice must be sought from the relevant agency in advance of any work (see Chapter 7).

Old plumbing

Old soil stacks made out of lead can be real works of art in themselves and are as much a part of a house's history as the building fabric, so don't replace them just for the sake of it. Modern replacements can look clumsy by comparison. Building inspectors can be quite sympathetic to old plumbing, providing it works.

Look after and keep any original bathroom fittings that are in the house as they are all part of the house's history and development. All sanitaryware can be overhauled when the need arises. You may have to research to find the right person to carry out the work, who is able to distinguish between appropriate as opposed to damaging repairs.

As bathroom fittings only really became available from around the 1870s onwards, you may possess first edition fittings and it is wise to preserve their short history as much as possible. While the main fittings may remain, the extras such as opaque white glass splash-backs and shelves have often been removed, so retain any that you may still have as they are becoming a rarity.

Most bathroom fittings were made in white before about the 1950s, then they went through a range of colours before arriving back at white again at the end of the twentieth century. Changing the wall colour to enhance an existing bathroom suite involves less effort and disturbance than replacement fittings.

Plumbing leaks

Deciding what to do with leaks in old pipes will depend on where the leaks are and the visual impact of repairs. The options include fill and cover, if it is a pinhole leak, or cut out and replace a section. A plumber should be able to advise which is feasible depending on the material.

All sanitaryware, whether old or new, will require some maintenance to ensure that the fittings last well into the future. WCs, baths and showers can leak for years undetected before the full extent of the damage is exposed. Taps and toilet cistern overflows start to drip when the washers perish. The most difficult part of replacing the washer is taking the tap apart as it may be clogged with lime scale. Make sure you find a plumber who understands old taps, as it is easy to damage both taps and fittings in the process if care is not taken.

Bathroom showers

Shower enclosures have to be completely waterproof to avoid water getting into the fabric of an old house. This means that the tiling and the junction with the shower tray must be completely rigid, which may not sometimes be possible in old houses which inevitably move slightly. Hairline cracks can develop in the grouting and sealant at the junction with the shower tray and if the movement is more serious individual tiles may crack.

Modern power showers can be very efficient at pressure pumping water into these tiny cracks. As the water cannot dry out underneath the tiling, it stays within the fabric of the house and starts to cause decay. Usually leaking showers are only discovered when water staining is noticed elsewhere and traced back, by which time a considerable amount of water may have entered the fabric of the house.

The Edwardians were well aware of these problems when showers were very first used in homes. They sometimes used lead-lined trays in floors under wet areas, drained to an outside wall.

Frost and plumbing

If the temperature inside the house falls below zero then heating and water pipes can freeze. Water expands when it freezes and the pipes may then fail at the weakest point – which is often the joints. Minimise the risk of the temperature dropping below zero by ensuring that a frost thermostat will safely activate a suitable heating system if you are away from the house for any length of time.

Also ensure that all pipes especially external ones are protected from frost by pipe insulation. This is particularly important in unheated areas such as roof spaces, along external walls or under floors. Electric trace-heating tapes can be applied to pipes which are particularly vulnerable.

New electrical wiring chases

An enormous amount of damage can be inflicted on the original fabric of an old house where completely new locations for electrical sockets and light fittings are proposed. For the wire to reach the fitting, chases will often be demanded in original fabric and old floorboards lifted in order to conceal them.

Make the most use of existing wiring positions by increasing the number of sockets in a particular position (if the capacity of the wiring will stand it) rather than creating completely new locations. Reduce the impact of damage on the fabric by careful positioning of surface-mounted cables that will reduce the need to disturb the existing fabric. Remember that trying to chase a lath and plaster wall will collapse the laths.

Routes for external wiring can detract from architectural features, such as this very old former doorway.

New pipework routes

Where a new heating system or bathroom is being installed in an old house, damage can be caused to the original fabric if the pipework routes have not been carefully worked out in advance. For example where a proposed pipe runs across the line of the floor joists, the joists would have to be cut to allow the pipe to pass, weakening them, destroying original fabric and causing a number of floorboards to be lifted.

Conserving existing heat

Old houses were generally constructed with far lower levels of insulation than are now required by the building regulations for new houses. The heat loss from old buildings can therefore be greater than from modern houses (unless, perhaps, you are lucky enough to live behind thick cob walls under a thatched roof).

By modern standards, old buildings were designed with very little in the way of universal heating and the result is that they are far more likely to dry out and start to crack as a result of installing a modern central heating system.

The first thing to consider is how to keep the existing heat in the home. As most heat escapes through the roof of the house it is sensible to put insulation in the existing attics and roof spaces. However, if impermeable roofing underlay has been laid on the roof, you must be careful that insulation does not block up the existing ventilation to the roof at the eaves as this can lead to condensation building up and mould growing on roof timbers. Glass fibre insulation has been used for some time but mineral wool is more or less comparatively priced and is considered less of an irritant by some. New greener ideas, such as sheep's wool, are currently being evaluated.

Rooflights, depending on their size, can be responsible for a large amount of heat loss and ideally could be secondary-glazed for the winter at the very least. Fixing a blind would also help to reduce the heat loss.

If the windows have existing shutters, use them to keep the heat in. If the windows were designed to have shutters and these are missing, think about having new shutters made. All windows and external doors benefit from having curtains. Close them when it is getting dark to help retain the existing heat. Thermal linings are available to put between the fabric and the lining of curtains and blinds so it is sensible to use these to improve their effectiveness.

Keeping room doors closed so that heat doesn't escape will help conserve heat within particular rooms. Think about which rooms you use in winter. You may decide to heat one room well rather than two rooms less satisfactorily. Where you have a staircase without a door at the bottom, hanging a curtain over it would stop the warm air escaping up the staircase. On bright sunny winter days allow as much sunlight into the house as you can, so that these rooms may warm up during the day, while keeping north-facing curtains in unused rooms closed if you reasonably can.

Maximise the efficiency of the existing heating system by applying reflective aluminium foil strips immediately behind a radiator in front of an external wall, as this will reflect the heat from the radiator back into the room. Fit thermostatic radiator valves to the existing radiators, if suitable. Room thermostats and programmable timers, which can be set

Window shutters help keep heat inside an old house in winter as well as providing some security.

to vary on a day to day basis, can all contribute to improving the efficiency of the existing heating system or the comfort.

Wearing warmer clothes in winter does make a difference to how much heating is necessary. This was part of our ancestor's heating regime when they lived in these houses as they had to move from heated rooms through unheated areas, or might not get as close to the fire as they liked.

Remember that musical instruments and antique furniture can be damaged by central heating so keep them where they are not likely to get over-heated or dry out too much.

Installing new heating in the home

There are a variety of types of heating available, from night storage heaters and electric panel radiators to the more common boiler and radiator systems. The choice of heating is usually determined by the fuels available. Where a gas supply is present this is likely to be more convenient than using oil or liquid propane gas (lpg) which require a storage tank and deliveries. Electric heating, while less disruptive to the fabric of an old house to install, it is generally more expensive to run.

Installing a gas supply can cause a lot of upheaval, depending on where the supply has to come from. But, like electricity, once it is there it is readily available. There is a legal requirement under the building regulations for all gas fire installations to have permanent ventilation into the room in which the appliance is used. These must not be blocked up since they ensure that there is enough oxygen to keep both the fire and the occupants alive.

Under-floor and ducted warm air heating are not usually very appropriate or suitable for old buildings, because they can require a lot of original fabric to be removed to facilitate the installation of ducts.

Paraffin heaters and portable gas heaters create a lot of water vapour in use, contributing to condensation problems unless sufficient ventilation is available. Introducing a new source of water vapour is unwise as it means there is more potential for damp to get into the fabric of the house.

Flue liners

These are a usual requirement if you are putting a gas-fire or new solid fuel appliance into any of the existing fireplaces, as the flue has to be impervious to combustion gases. There are two problems usually associated with installing flue liners in old houses.

Firstly, old chimney flues may have unusual bends and other surprises in them, so that physically fitting a flue liner down a chimney is often a difficult task. It is not uncommon as a result of a continuous liner being stuck somewhere that a large hole has to be made in the chimney wall to remove the flue liner and reinstate it. Similar problems can be experienced where sectional liners are used. Substantial damage to the fabric of the house can be caused during installation.

The second method of installing a flue liner involves an elongated balloon being placed down the flue and inflated. When positioned, concrete is poured down the flue around the sides of the balloon. A mass of rigid concrete hanging inside a crumbly chimney does not seem a particularly happy situation and it is possible that many have been installed without sufficient regard to the future integrity of the chimney. The newly solid chimney may no longer settle in the way it used to in harmony with the surrounding house.

Wood-burning stoves

These can be very effective at heating rooms in old houses and consequently have become very popular. As a result some problems have
come to light which means they must be installed and used with great
care. Some fire brigades now discourage the use of wood burning stoves
in thatched houses as it is believed that the chimney can overheat to the
point where combustion may occur in the thatch.

These stoves also require sturdy flue liners to be fitted in a chimney,
and installing these may sometimes be problematic. Because substancial
heat is generated in the flue, the chimney bricks may be exposed to considerable changes in temperature.

Wood-burning stoves require plenty of storage space for logs and
access to a ready supply of timber. Wood cannot be used as fuel if you
live in a smoke control area so contact the local environmental health
department for more information.

Ventilation

Old houses need to be kept well ventilated in order to minimise the
amount of water vapour entering the fabric. If this moisture is allowed to
build up it can ultimately lead to decay. Ventilation is usually already
present in old houses via a number of routes and it is unwise to be over-
zealous in blocking these up, otherwise the circulation of air will be
inhibited and any moisture in the fabric will not be able to dry out.

Fireplaces, where the flue has not been blocked up, are a very useful
source of ventilation and in summer, chimney stacks can contribute to
beneficial ventilation and cooling of the home.

Other useful sources of ventilation are the gaps around existing windows and doors that enable air to circulate and even overflow pipes from
toilet cisterns can allow air to circulate. There is a fine balance involved
in allowing the right amount of air into the home in order to combat
condensation, while keeping the occupants warm.

Since the advent of central heating the many household draughts
which usefully fuelled old open fires have been systematically tracked
down and sealed up. This has had a side effect in that airborne water
vapour has fewer opportunities to be vented.

Minimise the amount of water penetrating the fabric of an old house
through airborne moisture in order to avoid the onset of decay. The

high-risk areas in any house are kitchens and bathrooms where a lot of steam can be generated.

Simple measures like opening windows or keeping doors ajar will help. Also leaving draughts around doors and windows will help dissipate some of the hot damp air. (The building regulations now provide for trickle vents in new windows and mechanical extract fans in new kitchens and bathrooms).

It is sensible not to block up chimney flues, so that air can circulate freely and remove moisture-laden air from the internal environment. Even if the fireplace has gone, there is likely to be an airbrick to permit ventilation. Experimental 'green' buildings recently adopted a system of passive stacks for ventilation. These are in effect, open chimneys which are already present in most old houses.

A mechanical solution to poor ventilation is extract fans, but they can be difficult to locate aesthetically on external walls and affect the external character of a listed house, so listed building consent may be necessary.

Condensation

Condensation can be a problem for all ages of houses. It is moisture-laden warm air coming into contact with a cold surface so that the moisture converts to water droplets. If that cold surface is within the thickness of the wall, additional problems of decay follow. Where condensation is a problem and cannot be tackled in other ways then a de-humidifier can be used to extract moisture from the existing air. They are not really a long-term solution and other ways of using ventilation and heating should be considered.

Trying to avoid dramatic changes of temperature within an old house will help combat the problem of condensation. The peaks and troughs in the heating cycle can be smoothed out by the use of background heating to reduce the troughs. The right balance between heating and ventilation often requires fine-tuning rather than dramatic changes to combat condensation effectively.

Underpinning

Underpinning is where new foundations are introduced under existing walls. In old buildings partial underpinning can be a problem, because the underpinned part can remain rock-solid while the rest continues to move more freely as it would naturally. Even if this difference is very slight it can be enough to crack and distort the house.

The same problem can occur where a new extension is built on brand new deep foundations adjoining an old house with little or no foundations. It would be prudent to design a joint between the two parts of the building to accommodate such movement.

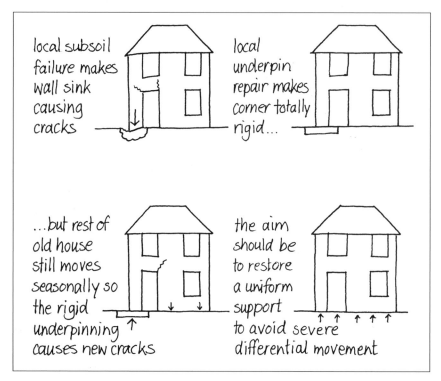

Potential adverse effects of underpinning.

Salvage yards

While some items have a legitimate reason for being in salvage yards, others may be there as a result of another old building being plumbered.

Salvage yards clearly represent recycling, which is good in principle, but not all recycling is done without compromise to the total sum of historic building conservation. It can also discourage new production, as while stocks are still available of old stone slates, for example, re-opening of old quarries or opening new ones is not a priority.

6

Alterations and extensions

Before considering how you might go about altering and extending an old house, the current situation with old buildings needs to be explored first. An old house that has survived as a genuine and attractive example of a past style has done so because it has not been altered out of recognition. The best examples have come down to us with the minimum of alteration and only necessary and sympathetic repairs. Where houses have been extended, some of the additions may not necessarily be as sympathetic to the original building as they might have been.

Of course adaptation over time is a natural part of a house's history and many buildings have been altered or extended over the years. Universally, the last major adaptations undertaken were the installation of internal WCs and bathrooms, together with electricity and central heating. In the past, alterations may have been made to buildings because of government taxes such as the window tax. This was first introduced in 1696 and only finally repealed in 1851 and led to the blocking of many windows.

Nowadays there are two significant differences with the past concerning alterations, one is the motivation for alterations and the other is about the methods used. In the past houses were generally altered and extended to meet necessary improvements in basic human needs such as health, hygiene, privacy and comfort. These days alterations are less about basic needs and more about personal choice.

Until the time that internal bathrooms were being installed, the vocabulary of the small builder extended to more or less the same tools, skills and materials that had been used for hundreds of years. There was no demand for producing something that jarred with an old house –

because there was little capability to do so. Even changes to follow fashion were limited by the same technical terms.

Now traditional materials have been supplemented by new variations and components which enable even the smallest builder to make a big statement on an old house and its environment – picture windows, long-spanning beams, plastics, earth-moving equipment, chemical pigments, artificial slates and tiles and so on. This new equipment has made redundant the use of local materials that gave a locality its architectural character.

For these reasons planning legislation is being used to control the ongoing development of old houses. If it were not there, the small number of historic houses left to us as a nation could rapidly dwindle to nothing.

The British Standards Institution produced a guidance document *BS 7913: The Principles of the Conservation of Historic Buildings* in 1998, which explores this further. It can be purchased from the BSI, or may be available at reference libraries.

Where a group of houses read as a composition it is important not to alter one house so that it stands out.

Priorities

Instigating alterations or extensions to an old house may seem more attractive as they are more visible, while repairs and maintenance, if they are carried out carefully, are hardly noticeable at all. Starting on alterations or extensions first can exhaust the financial resources before you have even begun to think about repairs; and leaving these until later will be a false economy. For example, a missing tile or a blocked down-pipe costs little to repair but can give rise to many thousands of pounds worth of repairs if ignored. So, safeguard the future of an old house by starting with careful repairs and maintenance first.

Design guidelines

Some councils produce guidance notes and diagrams on what types of extensions may be acceptable to different types of old houses. The conservation officer at the local or county council will usually be able to give you an indication of what types of extension are likely to be acceptable for your particular type of house.

How do alterations and extensions need to be approached?

All old houses and their individual situations are different, so each building has to be treated according to its own merits. However, the same general principle applies in all situations. The original fabric must be retained, so that the structure, character and appearance of an old house are not compromised.

Carefully thought through alterations should not detract from the existing shape or proportions of the home. Maintaining the shape of the roof profiles as well as the appearance of doors and windows is therefore important.

The interior is just as important to the history of the house and any proposed alterations will need to ensure that the internal integrity is respected and retained.

How and where to extend the house

New extensions, if designed to be in keeping with the rest of the house will not dominate or dwarf the original house. They need to be very carefully sited so they do not obscure or detract from existing features. A new sensitively designed extension is more likely to increase the value of the house.

Connection of the new extension to the old house is equally important. Making an existing window opening into a door would destroy less original fabric than creating a completely new door opening, perhaps incorporating the original window into the new work.

There are no precise answers as to how to design extensions or alterations as each old house and its situation is different. In practice if new elements are well-designed and detailed and carefully sited so that they do not dominate the existing house or detract from its character, they are more likely to receive a favourable response from the planners and conservation officers than when forcing an old house to be something it is not.

The effects an extension can have on an old house

While it is possible to construct a new extension with the same types of materials that were used on the original house, some of the ways in which a new extension has to be constructed will be different. This is because all new building work has to comply with the current building regulations (however, current government guidance PPG 15 does allow for flexibility).

Compliance with the building regulations can mean that, for example, new extensions require foundations that are built to a certain standard and this is dependent on local soil conditions. The depth or type of foundations will vary depending on these conditions.

Old buildings were constructed with much simpler, often shallow, foundations. While both types of foundation are appropriate for their respective periods, problems can arise where different types of building construction techniques meet.

Differential settlement is the technical term for resultant movement when a new building is built next to an existing building of whatever age. There is a possibility of the new and old moving differently to one another. This may result in cracks developing between the two builds. However, it is generally preferable to allow the builds to move independently, as trying to tie the two elements together could result in even more damage.

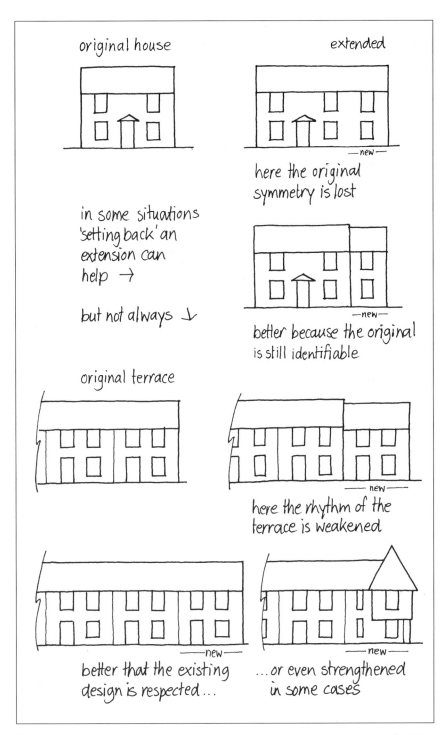

Treatment of extensions: Extending a house or adding a building to a group; some considerations.

a link can help articulate an extension
and reduce the amount of disturbance
to the existing wall

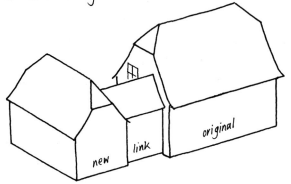

adopt design details from the existing eg:
roof profiles and 'swept' eaves, materials,
window proportions and design

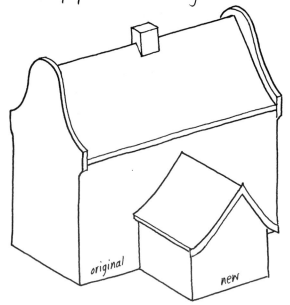

this simple rear extension is designed
to be subservient - so here it is perhaps
better not to have copied the grand gables

Treatment of extensions: Some more design considerations.

Conservatories

From both an historical and aesthetic point of view large conservatories are not necessarily appropriate for all old houses, especially as many houses pre-date the idea of conservatories but also the ability to absorb them comfortably. A rectory might have had one, but a crofter's cottage might have only ever run to a glazed lobby.

There are also physical constraints as to where a conservatory can be attached to an old house, so that existing elements such as roofs and windows are not compromised. The available locations are further diminished by the preference for a sunny aspect.

The types of materials used for conservatories also have an effect on detailing and appearance and how it relates. Materials that were traditionally available, like timber and glass, are more appropriate to historic settings than the more recently available materials like PVCu, aluminium and polycarbonate.

Where appropriate, a small, well-designed conservatory made of timber is more likely to gain planning and listed building consent (if the house is listed) than the recent fashion for a large additional living space.

Speak to the local conservation officer who should be able to advise you as to what may be acceptable in terms of size and location before you are tempted towards anything over-ambitious.

There are special building regulations surrounding conservatories designed to reduce the amount of heat-loss from them, so an application for building regulations approval is likely to be necessary.

7

Preventative measures and wildlife

Old houses, like any other buildings, can be subject to a number of unexpected circumstances, so it is advisable to ensure that appropriate preventative measures are in place to try and reduce or minimise the potential risks.

A sensible starting point is to record what already exists so that if a disaster occurs, you do at least have a documentary record. Although it is comparatively rare that a house is burnt to the ground, creating a photographic record or video ensures that there is some evidence available in the event of more minor damage or theft.

These would need to cover furnishings, architectural details and anything else that would be relevant if the house ever needed to be re-built or lost features or items replaced. Once created, the photographs or video should be kept up to date so that changes are recorded, then stored at another secure location, a relative's house perhaps.

Fire precautions during construction work

A number of major fires in old buildings have been linked to building work being carried out at the time. Hot work is the term used for any work on a building site, which requires the use of a naked flame, for example using a blow lamp, or a heat-producing appliance. Any use of naked flames should be avoided, when work is being carried out on an old house, as a basic safety precaution.

There are usually so many unknown voids and crevices that might be filled with flammable materials, like old bird's nests, that it is not worth taking the risk. Most conservation bodies have a blanket prohibition on hot work or, where there is absolutely no choice, strict guidelines are enforced together with fire-watching procedures. These ensure that work takes place early in the day and is finished many hours before the site is vacated.

There are usually ways to overcome hot work by pre-fabricating welded joints to pipes and leadwork off-site and by wet-sanding windows rather than using blow lamps. The latter is best avoided anyway, as the fumes from burning paint can be damaging to health, and might risk damaging the glass.

Electrical wiring

Old electrical wiring can be dangerous of course, but even new wiring can become a potential fire-hazard without warning, for example if the insulation around cables has been chewed by mice or if it overloads and is buried in thick roof insulation where it can heat up.

As there is the potential for greater fire risks in an old house, it is sensible to introduce safety measures wherever possible. Many fires have started as a result of faulty wiring, which with early warning protection devices in place could have been identified. It is a sensible precaution to have the electrical system checked over by a NICEIC (National Inspection Council for Electrical Installation Contracting) approved electrical contractor.

There are two varieties of safety trip switches, that can usually be added onto existing fuse boards, called MCBs (miniature circuit breakers) and RCDs (residual current devices) and these should trip out to alert you to potential problems. MCBs are trip-switches that replace the old-fashioned fuse-wire. RCDs (once called earth leakage circuit breakers) can, at certain ratings, reduce the risk of fatal electric shock and in some countries they are a requirement – for example in this country for certain exterior power applications on new houses.

A series of combination switches (in place of old-fashioned fuses at the fuseboard) which incorporate the features of both MCB and RCD would usually be able to detect and respond to a broad range of problems on each circuit and may even help reduce the risk of fire in some circumstances.

Check all electrical appliances to make sure that the leads are not damaged and that there are no exposed wires where the flex comes out of the plug or goes into the appliance and that hot lamps and elements are well away from surfaces. Test older appliances as there comes a time when these things, such as 1950s electric heaters with their perished

rubber wires and albestos insulators, may need to be given an hon-
ourable retirement as collectible curios.

Renew any wiring that has been bound up with electrical tape or
looks like it has been repaired in the past. Make sure that correctly rated
fuses are used in all plug-tops and that these are appropriate to the
appliances the plug is being used with, and any flex that serves it. Low-
consumption appliances, like most table lamps and radios, do not
require the full capacity of a 13 amp fuse in the plug, a 3 amp fuse usually offers more appropriate protection. Consult an electrician.

Down-lighters

There are two main concerns about the use of down-lighters in the ceilings of old houses unless certain additional fire precautions are taken.
Where a hole is cut in a ceiling to install one of these recessed fittings
the fire resistance of the ceiling is breached, and when in use these fittings create a build-up of heat in the confined area within the ceiling
void. All this is much more dangerous if there is thatch above. Loose
laid insulation over these units will cause a dangerous build-up of heat
and risk to cables.

The use of these fittings should be avoided in old houses where lath
and plaster ceilings have to be cut, and the cut laths are left unsupported
and the ceiling is weakened.

Open fires

Chimneys must be swept regularly, as the build-up of soot in a chimney
can fuel a hidden fire that is difficult to extinguish. Old house chimneys
often have large hidden cavities that need special care to clean out
(these occur after fireplaces have been reduced in size when coal took
over from logs).

Open fires also require airflow to function, so rooms must not be
completely air-tight.

Furniture and fire-retardant fabrics

All new and re-upholstered pieces of furniture are required to incorporate
fire retardant material. Furniture manufactured between about 1950 and
1983 is likely to be of a construction that has been identified as of particular concern from a fire-risk point of view. Think very carefully about
using this type of furniture in an old house, particularly where matches

or cigarettes could start a fire. If necessary relegate it to a safer environment or have it re-upholstered, specifying fire-retardant materials.

Fire retardant materials are available for curtains so wherever possible use these materials to reduce the risk of fire.

Gas appliances

All gas appliances should be regularly checked over. Landlords are required to have gas boilers checked annually, where properties are rented out on leases that are less than seven years in length.

Gas equipment should be installed and serviced by properly qualified personnel. The industry offers a registration scheme under the CORGI name (Council for Registered Gas Installers).

Thatch

If you have a thatched house, your house insurers may provide you with safety guidelines or requirements. Trying to eliminate electrical wiring from the roof space is a sensible precaution. If this is not possible then wiring must be tested regularly. Suitable smoke alarms should be installed in the roof space as well as elsewhere in the house and they need to be inter-linked to sound in the main house or on the intruder alarm.

Make sure there is a hose long enough to reach the roof, and access to an outside tap with the correct tap connector, in case it is needed in an emergency. A visible spark arrestor mesh on the chimney can be re-assuring if you have open fires, though some fire authorities find that if not properly maintained it can produce other serious risks.

Reducing the risks – general fire safety equipment

Smoke detectors – either wired into the existing mains electrical or alarm systems or alternatively a battery-operated detector installed where they can be heard. Some can be interlinked so that they all sound together. If using battery operated alarms replace batteries on a regular basis in accordance with manufacturer's instructions. They will not save lives without working batteries.

Kitchens – are a high-risk area for fires. Fix a fire blanket container to the wall in the kitchen between the cooker and the exit door. A powder fire extinguisher is a worthwhile additional safeguard. However fire officers may prefer people to get out of the house, rather than trying to fight a fire themselves as fires bring other risks such as gas explosions.

Water – think where the nearest source is and make sure a hose is available. Do not use water on electrical appliances. Specialist extinguishers are available for oil or similar risks.

Protection – store valuables in a fire and waterproof safe and memorise the security number. Keep room doors shut at night.

Floods

In the event of flooding take up all waterlogged carpets and anything else that will stop the house drying out. Lift a couple of floorboards where water has got into floor voids to allow air to circulate and help dry it out gradually. Beware of electric cables and appliances short-circuited by water.

Cellar floods

If the cellar walls and floor are of porous brick that have been laid in lime mortar with a limewash finish on the wall these are likely to dry out again more satisfactorily than if the walls have had an impervious paint finish applied to them.

Ensure that adequate ventilation is present so that water vapour from standing water can be removed from the area rather to prevent it penetrating ceiling timbers for example.

If it is necessary to drain standing water in the cellar, a cellar pump can be used, but it is likely that the water that is pumped away will be replaced by more water because of the water table being higher than the level of the cellar floor. When water is continually pumped from a cellar, it is likely to wash out particles of mortar in the cellar walls, so substantial water extraction could lead to a weakening of the structure.

Plumbing leaks

Turn the water off immediately. Remove all sodden materials and increase ventilation to the affected area to aid drying out, then deal with the leak itself. The tiniest pin-hole leak, if undetected for weeks, can saturate a large area. Be careful of ceilings if they have been saturated – especially plasterwork on laths which can have lost its key due to softening by water and be at risk of falling.

Late nineteenth-century and early twentieth-century architects drew on vernacular styles.

House insurance

Once an old house is damaged by whatever cause, it is too late to discover you have insured with a company that does not understand the special requirements of a listed or old building.

You may want to re-instate a finely carved oak staircase or a lath and plaster ceiling destroyed by fire. The local planning department may also want to insist that you do. However, you may find the insurers feel they can discharge their obligations by offering you the price of a plain wooden stair and a plasterboard ceiling. Check out your policy before this becomes an issue.

The value of the buildings you are insuring is usually the cost of re-building, which can be more that the purchase price as it may cost more to re-build an oak-framed thatched cottage than it cost to buy. Be clear with the insurer just what needs to be insured. Specialist insurers or companies with departments geared to old properties may be more inclined to arrange such areas of cover.

If you are anticipating having building work done to an old house, you must advise the insurer, otherwise you may find that the cover is invalid during the building works. Tell them what type of contract you or the architect are using with the contractor – this will help them understand the risk.

Security

An old house may or may not be sturdier than a new property. What it is less likely to be, if it is still as built, is as resistant to break-in as a modern home.

Locks have developed in complexity and security, particularly recently in response to insurance requirements. A five or seven lever mortice deadlock is very difficult to open by comparison with a basic mortice lock or simple rim-latch (the type almost universally found on front doors for half a century), but few burglars pick locks any more. A lock is only as good as the fixing it has into the door and frame, and that of the strength of the timber left around it.

Windows are even flimsier and glass only deters by the sound it makes when broken – little comfort in a remote house. It makes sense to upgrade all door locks where possible (this needs to be done with due regard to the fabric of any historic doors and windows, weighing up the amount of material to be removed and the visual and structural effect this will have). Don't settle for the locks on display at the DIY store if they don't fit well on the doors. They are selling to a mass market living in modern homes with standard doors. A little research can turn up a whole list of specialist security locks that will not damage the look and the fabric of the home – and protect it too.

Provide such catches and fastenings as the insurers require or the local crime prevention officer advises. But do be aware that security is their priority rather than a concern for damage could be inflicted on an old building as a result of carrying out the necessary work.

Keep sight of what you are about to do to the venerable old door or window. Insurance companies can issue their requirements without any knowledge of the physical condition of the property in question. Too many locks, or too big a lock might even weaken a door rather than strengthen it. If you are worried about this consult someone who has tackled this problem sensitively on old houses before or the crime prevention officer may be able to suggest alternative approaches to security.

Alarms

These start with simple DIY radio controlled systems involving the minimum of wiring (but often the maximum of battery replacement), up to complex networks of detectors permanently wired into the house and possibly connected by a telephone line to a remote staffed control centre. The control centre then undertake to contact the police if certain conditions are met by any alarm they detect.

As with other installations in the home, you need to consider the damage that running wires and concealing detectors is going to do to historic fabric. In this respect, radio systems are preferable and the systems available will no doubt rapidly develop in the coming years.

Common sense

You can help reduce the risk of the home being burgled in the first place by being sensible about locking up, even when you are at home. You may be insured but that cannot compensate for the inconvenience. Remember that, with the exception of specialist antiques thieves, the most likely target is money and easily sold consumer goods. Arrange the furniture so that enticing valuables are not visible to passers-by. If there is Georgian glass in the sash window it is less replaceable than the high-technology equipment that might tempt someone to smash it.

If there is any doubt in would-be burglars' minds about whether you are at home or whether you have an alarm – and it looks like you have got decent locks, then they will most likely go and find somewhere less well protected.

Automatically controlled lighting, both internally and externally can be a good deterrent, but remember to think carefully about where to site external lights as these can be extremely annoying to road users or neighbours.

Make sure that things like ladders and garden tools are locked away so that they can't be used to help carry out a burglary. Speak to the local crime prevention officer who should be able to keep you up to date with targets of crime in the area, methods and deterrents.

Safety precautions when working on old buildings

Most accidents connected with DIY involve ladders, so make sure that a ladder is strong enough for the proposed work and is firmly positioned and tied at a safe angle before being used. Wear shoes with a good grip.

There are numerous accidents each year involving tower scaffolds that have not been properly erected or stabilised. The Health and Safety Executive produce an information sheet on these. Safety goggles, masks and gloves are sensible for most DIY. Other protective gear is essential for using some power equipment or working at heights.

Hazards in old buildings

There may be some hazardous materials already in existence in an old house. These materials were, at the time of their original use, not thought to be a problem and it is only with greater understanding and knowledge that these materials have now been identified as potentially dangerous.

Poisonous substances were sometimes used as dyes, inks and pigments and there is even a possibility of finding anthrax spores in certain historic fabric. However, perhaps the two most likely harmful materials that old house owners may encounter are lead and asbestos.

Lead paint

Lead paint can now only be used on Grade I and II* listed buildings and scheduled ancient monuments, providing special permission has been granted by English Heritage in England or Cadw in Wales. In Scotland the same applies to Category A buildings, so contact Historic Scotland and in Northern Ireland approval must be obtained from the Environment and Heritage Service.

Lead-based pigments were widely used in paints until the 1960s so it is likely that all old houses have been painted with it at some time in the past. Lead paint was initially discouraged from children's toys for fear of ingestion and the same hazard came to be recognised to be present in building paintwork.

Before carrying out any work to old paint read the advice leaflets, which are usually available from the paint supplier or environmental health department at the local council. Lead testing kits are usually available from paint suppliers.

All old paint where it needs to be rubbed down before being over painted, should be prepared by hand by wet sanding as the dust particles are harmful if inhaled. The use of power sanders on old buildings is in any case inadvisable as they can do a great deal of damage to old joinery. Dry sanding can create a harmful lead-rich dust (and may damage glass).

Burning off old paint with a blow-lamp causes toxic fumes. It is also prudent never to use a blow-lamp or a hot air gun on an old building as there is a greater fire risk associated with working on them. Any nearby glass may also crack from the heat generated.

For further information see the Department for Environment, Food and Rural Affairs (DEFRA) website.

Lead mains water pipes

Lead can appear in drinking water from lead pipes that are used within or near the house. Before undertaking disruptive investigation or replacement it might be wise to have the drinking water tested for actual lead content since there is a pragmatic view that in hard water areas the lead pipes line themselves with limescale. Proper testing should help clarify individual circumstances. Lead was used in some solder for copper pipes until a few decades ago.

Asbestos in old (and not-so-old) buildings

Until it was recognised as a health-hazard and banned late in the twentieth century, asbestos was seen as a versatile building material widely used since Victorian times. Its fire-resistance was its chief advantage but its ability to bind and reinforce other materials plus its use as thermal insulation, were also important.

Asbestos becomes a danger to health when it is disturbed and tiny airborne particles are inhaled, causing fatal lung disease. It was used in many forms – hard asbestos cement in boards and rainwater goods, pipe, heater and boiler insulation as compounds, sheets or bandages, accessories on heat appliances from oven-door gasket rope to fireplace caulking, in finishes from textured paints and flexible sheets to floor and roof tiles, and from fillers to wall plugs, to name just a few. It will keep turning up for many years. Just about every old house will have had some asbestos used in it at some time, even if it was only an ironing-board mat. Old electric heaters, particularly storage heaters, may have used asbestos as insulation. The makes and models of suspect storage heaters are listed – ask the local council.

Asbestos has many forms and colours, some varieties being more harmful than others. If found it should be sealed off (and if appropriate, gently dampened) as soon as discovered to avoid the dust being inhaled. The local authority should be able to advise initially on how to find out about identification procedures and safe removal, which is usually a job for licensed specialists working with special protection.

Asbestos can pose a serious risk if mishandled. Its safe removal can be an expensive and time-consuming part of other works so it is necessary to establish its existence before embarking on any old house project.

For further information see the Department for Environment, Food and Rural Affairs (DEFRA) website.

Conserving the existing built environment and materials

There is now much more concern about conserving natural resources and caring for the environment and these principles are parallel with those of responsibly looking after old buildings.

Old houses are eminently repairable, often using little more than mediaeval technology. Ultimately, (though demolition is to be avoided) they are also eminently recyclable. Bricks can be re-used if set in lime mortar, while old carpentry joints can often be dismantled. When recycling, it helps that many building components have been made in standard sizes for a long time, such as bricks, roof tiles, slates and even plumbing goods, ensuring that re-use and interchangeability are feasible.

The vast majority of old houses were built from reasonably local materials avoiding transportation wherever possible. Old houses were built without using processed materials rich in the environmentally harmful substances, which use a lot of energy to produce them. The simple natural materials of old buildings might be expected to have a better health record than complex modern compounds.

In addition, our ancestors efforts to understand insulation, ventilation, humidity control and the daylighting of interiors are now being rediscovered in the interests of energy-saving and comfort. New technology and understanding coupled with centuries of experience can provide a leaner and greener building methodology.

Natural as opposed to synthetic products are most compatible with the existing traditional low technology natural materials found in old buildings. Additionally, from an environmental point of view, retaining the maximum amount of existing fabric means that less new resources are used to replace them.

There have been a number of recent developments in environmentally friendly building products, from building blocks that do not contain concrete, to insulation that uses sheep's wool instead of highly manufactured products.

When purchasing any materials for an old house think about what they are made from as well as how they will look. There are alternatives to applying toxic insecticides and fungicides. Modern materials like PVC, which is often used for rainwater and drainage pipes are being challenged in terms of their environmental credentials and alternatives are available that can be chosen to reflect different values.

Even kitchen units are not safe from an environmental audit as for example some of the ingredients of glues in particle-boards are said by some to have a higher environmental impact than solid timber.

There are many materials still available today that are likely to be phased out in the future because the material and methods used to produce these are perceived as harmful both to the environment and the end user once the products are installed.

Wildlife

Various forms of wildlife may sometimes inhabit roofs and voids.

Birds – wild birds, their nests and eggs are protected under Part 1 of the Wildlife and Countryside Act 1981 and it is an offence – except in certain situations which include pest species – to remove or destroy a bird's nest while it is in use or being built. If removing redundant nests from inside the roof space after the birds have flown make sure that the access route to the nest is sealed off with wire netting. This should allow ventilation, but not birds, into the roof space in future. Where pigeons have been allowed to enter a roofspace, their droppings (guano) are a health hazard, and health and safety precautions should be taken on removal.

Mice and rats – try to establish where they are entering the house and block up the holes to deter them. They are good at climbing and love burrowing in roof insulation and gnawing electric cables.

Bees and wasps – colonies are often found in roof spaces and voids.

Grey squirrels – if they get into a roof space, they can make a lot of noise and can chew wiring and timber. They also like roof insulation for their nests. Entice or wait for squirrels to leave their chosen area and block up their entrance to the roof otherwise they will return. Squirrels don't like mothballs so these can be used as a deterrent, If you catch a grey squirrel, as they are not native to Britain and are currently regarded as vermin, they cannot legally be released back into the wild.

Bats –these are protected by the Wildlife and Countryside Act 1981. It is an offence to harm or handle a bat, or obstruct or destroy their access to any place they are using. Bats return to use the same roosting sites each year so these areas are protected even when the bats are not there.

Bats are usually seen flying at dusk. The most likely place for their roosts is in roof spaces or outbuildings. They can be surprisingly tiny and can access barely noticeable chinks in roofs. The location of droppings under ridge-boards, hips and around chimneys or gable ends may give you clues as to their presence. Bat droppings look very similar to those of mice. Bats droppings can be flaked exposing fragments of insects, their principal diet.

If you are not sure whether you have bats, contact the local bat group through the Bat Conservation Trust who can carry out a bat watch to establish if they are present. Once you have established that you have bats and if you are planning to carry out building or timber treatment work, you must consult the relevant country agency well before any building works start. They can advise you as to the particular situation.

8

Interiors and their care

The interior of an old house will explain, to an experienced eye, how its history has developed over the years. Character is usually created by what already exists in an old house rather than being applied subsequently. Many people mistakenly believe that removing the original plaster to expose brick or stone walls, for example, will enhance the character of an old house, when in fact it is more likely to destroy its authenticity.

Stripping paint from existing features, such as doors or other painted woodwork, creates another set of visual problems. The timber used to make doors often had knots, irregular grain and other imperfections that would be covered up by paint. Removing the paint to expose the wood produces a different visual result from that originally intended.

The most vulnerable items are those that are easily removable, from doors down to doorknobs, but over zealous stripping can easily destroy unsuspected wall paintings (which can be found in any size of house or cottage).

In Victorian times many buildings, churches and cathedrals in particular, were restored to the Victorians' interpretation of mediaeval buildings. These buildings are now seen as Victorian as their mediaeval content has been masked. Reacting against this practice of conjectural restoration, William Morris established the Society for the Protection of Ancient Buildings in 1877. This society has been actively pursuing the careful care and repair of old buildings ever since.

Caring for the fabric of the interior

The interior finishes of an old house should be breathable in the same way that the exterior fabric should be, in order to allow the structure to absorb and then evaporate moisture uniformly. Finishes and floor coverings that are impermeable can interfere with this regime, leading to problems.

Wall paintings, or another form of decoration, may be discovered in an old cottage, so be vigilant when work is being carried out in case something interesting is unwittingly destroyed.

The effects of alterations to interiors

Alterations to the interiors of an old house can easily, and often inadvertently, destroy or damage the character and fabric of an old house. Even when intending to re-instate finishes, such as re-plastering masonry walls or re-painting wooden panelling that have been stripped, then these may also require consent if the house is listed, as they may be classed as alterations to the existing fabric.

Even if the house is not listed the same criteria apply to any internal alterations you are considering. The destruction or removal of original fabric or features would be likely to devalue the overall special historical quality of an old house.

While a lot of focus is placed on repairing an old house to keep the weather out, the interiors are the areas where most time is spent enjoying an old house as a home once the rest of the work is complete.

What style for the interior?

The interiors of old houses usually have so many existing features that the style already exists and needs only to be enhanced by careful choices of colours and textiles. The skill of interior decoration in old houses is to choose colour schemes, furnishings and fabrics that complement the existing, rather than trying to give an old house a face-lift possibly destroying some of the original character in the process.

One of the charms of old houses is that some existing features may not seem to conform to current expectations. For example, a corner fireplace may not be exactly what you want but it can be emphasised as a quirky feature rather than trying to tidy things up and move it to a more conventional position.

Another tempting strategy that does not usually work well with old houses is trying to take them back in time. Creating an interior that predates the construction of the house is misleading, as is trying to take the interior back to Victorian times, for example. There will always be compromises and errors. An historically correct interior would, in most cases, require no running hot water or electricity. These are modern conveniences that most people are not willing to sacrifice for the sake of perceived authenticity.

Historical research

If you want to find out something in particular about an old house or about the colour schemes that would have been used, there are a variety of sources available. Start by looking at the further reading list at the end of this book. There are national amenity societies that probably cover the dates of the house.

Often by examining the history of an old house and its features, you will be able to identify the dates at which certain things happened to the house. Re-cycling was popular in previous centuries as modern methods of disposal were not available, so almost anything could have been brought into a house from nearby if the opportunity arose.

Where relevant dates have been established for a house or for a room within it, then the colour schemes and materials available at those dates can be identified. Current manufacturers of wallpaper, paint and fabrics produce historically matched colours and designs for particular periods although many contemporary colours and designs are suited to old houses. By studying the historical ranges you can get a feel for which colours were common and which colours rare. It is still necessary to be careful about vapour-permeability when selecting and using such products since historic colours are available in conventional modern paints as well as traditional ones.

What to do about a missing feature

Where features have already been removed, a fire surround for example, our instinct may be to go to a salvage yard and find a suitable period replacement. Commissioning a new fireplace to a traditional or new design that will enhance the room is a better solution and allows you to make a personal contribution to the history of the house in the process.

Previous alterations

Whether an old house has features from the 1860s or the 1970s they are equally of value. Items from the recent past will almost certainly come back into fashion so they may soon be revered rather than ripped out. By retaining previous alterations you will be preserving them for future generations to enjoy, and you could save yourself money. Try to utilise the features and spaces as found.

Getting help with colour schemes

If you would like help in making choices for your colour schemes, curtains and fabrics, then an interior designer is usually able to help choose what is appropriate for the house. But it is vitally important to choose someone who understands and has successful experience of working with old houses.

As so many features usually already exist in an old house, the skill of an interior designer is to highlight these and create a scheme that harmonises rather than competes with these features.

Interior elements

Internal features and elements can often be damaged or destroyed where insufficient thought is given to them before any work is started. The following sections identify particular interior elements and care considerations.

If in doubt about what to do in a particular situation speak to an architect or building surveyor who is experienced and knowledgeable in the care and conservation of old buildings.

Plaster ceilings

Plaster ceilings were often painted with distemper until the 1950s and 1960s when emulsion paints became popular. Limewash and whiting (made from chalk) were generally used on the ceilings and walls in out-buildings before then and these earlier paint finishes are more likely to survive in buildings that were redecorated less often.

Because these earlier paint finishes have a powdery finish, plastic emulsion paint does not adhere to them very well and tends to peel off. Decorators may offer you sealers to enable over-painting with vinyl paint, but these trap in the damp, whereas using distempers can allow the walls and ceilings to breathe and create a characterful surface finish.

Soft distemper, limewash and whiting are still available today and are all very good for ceilings as they allow the surface to breathe. They also reflect light in a much more subtle and pleasing way than modern emulsions.

There is a knack to removing emulsion paint but often a wallpaper scraper angled very close to the ceiling will remove it. Where a room has been subject to steam, such as kitchens or bathrooms, it may not be so easy to remove.

Cornices and ceiling roses

Decorative cornices and ceiling roses may lose their details where many years of over painting have begun to obscure the details. It is likely the majority of the early layers of paint are water-based, limewash or more often distemper. Where the details are clogged with paint and difficult to remove, try gentle steam stripping to remove the paint. Try a sample area in an inconspicuous place to see how it works before going further. Decorative details may also be softened by steam, so be extremely careful not to damage these when trying to remove the paint.

When sufficient paint has been removed for the details to again be visible, apply a soft distemper or limewash over the surfaces.

Ceiling timbers

Ceiling timbers are rarely left untouched and may have been painted at some point in their history, otherwise they are best left as found. Where gloss paint, for example, has been applied in the recent past it may now be possible to remove this with some of the new techniques available.

Beams might have been painted for a reason, so paint removal may reveal some disfigurement, which may need to be covered over again or repaired.

In mediaeval times, many internal walls and beams were painted with decorative designs (even in apparently quiet humble dwellings), so careful investigation is necessary to be certain that nothing more than modern gloss paint will be removed if you go down this route.

The chemicals needed to remove the paint will depend on the type of paint. Generally, solvent-based removers are often able to remove modern types of paint, while alkaline removers can usually dissolve older oil-based paints. If you use paint-strippers, choose from among the products that are recognised to pose least human and environmental risk. It is sensible to carry out tests on small areas first to see what works before embarking on larger areas. Be sure to neutralise any chemicals afterwards.

Alternatively, mechanical removal can be achieved successfully with a recently developed vortex system of gently abrasive paint removal (as distinct from conventional sandblasting). This is best carried out in a vacant building as it causes a great deal of dust. While this technique is potentially able to strip paint without damaging timber, this depends entirely upon the ability of the operator. A skilled operator can strip even a soft timber like pine without leaving a hairy raised grain. Always get a sample carried out in advance to minimise the potential for disappointment and damage.

Listed building consent may be required where a house is listed, depending on the type of paint removal system to be used, but equally be aware that even if the house is not listed, you may still come across old and interesting paintwork.

Boxed-in ceiling timbers

Structural ceiling timbers were sometimes boxed-in by the Georgians and Victorians to give a less rustic look in certain rooms. This was also done in their new buildings. They often had bead mouldings at the edges where the covering timbers met. These casings form a part of the house's history showing its perceived elevation from a vernacular dwelling into something grander, and should not be removed to expose the beam. The timber on these boxings should be painted since the intention was to make them look less like timber and more like ceiling. These beams were traditionally often coated with soft distemper so that they blended in with the rest of the ceiling, rather than making a feature of them.

Brick and stone walls

Any original plaster that still exists should be kept so that the character and original fabric are maintained. However, where plaster has already been removed you have the option of covering up the wall with lime plaster again.

A decision can only be reached by weighing up each situation and judging the possible visual effects. Listed building consent may be necessary for this type of work where a house is listed.

Timber framing in walls

Where the timber framing is exposed, you are usually able to tell if it was originally intended. If rows of nail holes are present this is evidence that at some time in the past the wall was covered up. These nail holes indicate that timber laths were fixed to the framing for plaster to be applied over them at some point in the building's history.

What you do as a result of this discovery very much depends on each individual situation and weighing up the options available. If the timbers are to remain exposed, avoid applying varnishes or sealants as these could trap moisture in the timber.

Plastered walls

Even if old lime plaster sounds hollow in small areas on solid backgrounds, this is no reason for replacing it if no other defects are noticeable. Try to avoid replacing plaster or patching it unnecessarily. Cracks can be carefully filled so that they do not detract from the overall finish. What may look like a hopeless case can with skill be carefully transformed through careful grading using fine lime and sand mixes or fillers. Distemper and limewash are good at concealing visual flaws because they have body and do not aspire to a flat finish.

Wall tiles

Wall tiles were a Victorian favourite. There are many good copies of old pattern tiles available but because older buildings tend to move a bit, they are sometimes susceptible to cracking, so may not look as good as they could. The other problem with tiles is that they require a level background, which can be difficult to find unless of course the old house is Victorian.

Original Edwardian wall tiles give added character to this space.

Interiors like this need careful handling to avoid sacrificing interest for the sake of tidiness.

Modern internal plasters

Certain types of modern plasters can be unsuited to old buildings. Specific types of gypsum plaster can be especially problematic in old buildings, because they attract and retain damp. As there can be higher levels of dampness locally in old buildings the two are not readily compatible. Manufacturers recommend that certain types of plaster are unsuitable for use in potentially damp situations. Where plaster has been used and is causing a problem, it can usually be carefully removed and the wall re-plastered using traditional lime and sand plaster.

There are modern waterproof plasters and renders that may have been used in the past on old houses in conjunction with injected damp courses in order for guarantees to be issued. Providing that damp is no longer a problem these types of plaster are unfortunate but may be best left undisturbed. However, it is now considered unwise to knowingly introduce these modern waterproof plasters into an old building. In the past they may have been used in conjunction with aluminium foils and bituminous products to attempt to seal damp into walls. This is now seen as tackling only the symptoms.

Internal textured decorative finishes

During the 1960s and 1970s decorative products were available to give a textured finish and were liberally applied to many old buildings. These recent finishes can be carefully removed and repairs made to the original walls using similar materials to the original plaster. In removing the decorative finish, you may discover the reason why problems were covered up with a textured finish in the first place.

Some finishes were once made with asbestos added and if you are in any doubt you can have a sample tested. The local authority ought to be able to suggest how to go about this.

Difficult to remove finishes in non-critical locations can successfully be covered over (some textured finish manufacturers market an obliterating coating for this purpose).

Doors

Where old or original internal doors remain, these should be kept, as they are a part of the history of an old house. Old doors may have been cut down or increased in size to fit new openings as it was easier to recycle an existing door than to make a new one.

Slamming doors shut may cause cracks in both the doors themselves and the surrounding wood and possibly even the surrounding walls as well, so be gentle when closing doors, especially if they have glass panels in them.

Ironmongery – knobs, hinges, locks and finger plates

Old door handles are a part of the history of the doors and, carefully maintained, they should last a very long time and do not need to be replaced. Doorknobs are one of the early candidates for DIY replacement so you will be lucky if you still have many original ones left.

What if the handles have been replaced already? After iron and brass doorknobs, the next fashion was for the brown plastic, known as Bakelite. This was produced mainly between the mid-1920s and the 1960s. These in themselves are very collectable so retain any you have as they add to the history of the house.

All the metal fittings in the house, from doorknobs to hinges and window latches where they have not been replaced, are a small but important part of the history of an old house. While modern copies can now be bought, they do not have the patina of age and are only reproductions. Old hinges are often artworks in themselves, so when they begin to wear, repair them rather than replace them, as they are often contemporary with the door to which they are fixed. Sometimes worn hinges can be left in place and supplemented with additional matching ones.

Old door locks can be carefully maintained and looked after so that they remain in use indefinitely. Old locks can usually be repaired and new keys made even for the very oldest of locks. A rule of thumb that indicates the age of a door by the number of locks that it has had on it is one lock for each hundred years. As with any old fittings, they are part of the house's history and so, even if redundant, keep them to retain the history.

Make sure that the lock mechanism is protected from dampness and dust by a cover flap (escutcheon) over the keyhole on the external face of a door. Old locks can be maintained with graphite (soft pencil lead), avoid using oil or grease as these attract dirt, causing wear.

Fingerplates were often fitted above doorknobs to keep dirty finger marks and wear and tear at bay. Like doorknobs, they can be of brass, glass, wood, ceramic or Bakelite. Often these are missing because they became unfashionable when wipe clean gloss paints allowed modern houses to dispense with them.

You may be able to see an impression on the doors of various pieces of door furniture that have since been removed or replaced or where

This lock has been cleverly re-used upside down.

doors have been altered for re-use in other positions. These are not imperfections to be sanded smooth but records of the past, which will gain in interest with the passing years and maintain the character of an old house.

Previous colour schemes

Where the existing surface finishes are cut through, for example, where paint has been chipped or behind electrical fittings, you may be able to find clues of previous colour schemes. Be aware that you may be looking at undercoats, primers and colours that have changed with age. Paint samples can be analysed to get a clearer indication of the colours that can be dated accurately.

The colours for paint used on woodwork have changed through the centuries. The Georgians generally preferred lighter colours, while the Victorians loved dark colours and graining. As different colours were fashionable at different times it is often possible to get an indication of what these might have been by matching them to historical colour charts that are available from present day paint manufacturers.

Previous wallpapers

Any existing cupboards might reveal old wallpapers. Often spare rolls were used-up in cupboards, so they may indicate what was used in other rooms of the house. If walls have had emulsion paint applied to them, sometimes you can see that there are the lines of wallpaper underneath. Existing wallpaper was often painted over – most usually during the 1960s and 1970s. Clues about old papers may still be found under light switches for example.

If you do find fragments, there are some wallpaper manufacturers who specialise in historical papers and they may be able to identify the style and date and even have something similar in their current ranges. Keep any fragments of wallpaper with a note of where and when they were found as a historical record. You may later find another similar piece elsewhere in the house. Decorators sometimes wrote notes on a wall so keep a look out for any useful historical clues.

Internal woodwork

Recently there has been a fashion for stripped pine, which can extend to any item of joinery in the home – doors, windows, skirting boards and architraves. This is not a true reflection of history or of vernacular styles, unless the timberwork dates from mediaeval times and was meant to be seen in its raw state (in which case it would probably be oak and meticulously finished).

If you have a house where someone else has stripped the paint off the woodwork, you might consider re-painting it, to protect it and increase the light in the rooms. If the interiors of the timber window frames have been stripped, they can also reduce the amount of reflected light in the rooms. If all the joinery has had the paint removed it will be very difficult to gather information about the paint colours used previously, as most of the evidence will have gone. However, the removal of paint from timber is never total so you may discover traces of paint on closer inspection.

Woodwork painted prior to the 1960s may have been painted with lead paint and where re-decoration is involved, precautions are necessary (see Chapter 7). You will not be able to use lead paint to repaint joinery but there are gentler (and more traditional) paints available from specialists than the standard modern commercial paints.

Wooden floors

Avoid sanding timber floors as this removes the surface of boards and with it their history. Floorboards were usually not intended to be the dominant feature in a room and were often largely covered by rugs.

Varnishes, sealants and paints are best avoided on any type of floor finish as these can create an unnaturally glazed look which could be slippery and are likely to seal in dampness rather than allowing it to escape. Certain waxes and oils are suitable as they do not form a surface skin, but even these may cause the floor to be slippery if over-zealously applied.

The wider the floorboards, the older they usually are. Hardwoods, being less likely to curl, can be broader than softwoods. It is part of the charm and character of an old house to see where boards have been cut and re-laid in the past. While poor workmanship can be improved upon, it is better conservation to keep old floors and patch them, rather than replace them in a modernising attempt to over-tidy things.

Underneath the floorboards on the first floor you may find an early form of sound insulation, which can be made from a variety of materials depending on the part of the country. Avoid removing this as it was put there to reduce sound transmission, but be careful that cables do not run through it creating a fire risk.

Modern floorboards are produced in narrower widths to overcome curling, and are jointed to each other by a tongue and groove system to make them stronger. This was not easily available to our un-mechanised ancestors.

Wooden floors at ground floor level must have ventilation below the floorboards or they may be susceptible to dampness and rot. Check that the floor is adequately ventilated. Shrinkage gaps between floorboards can be filled with papier-mâché.

Lifting old floorboards can lead to damage, as they are usually not easy to lever up in one piece, so only carry this out where there are no other alternatives. Where old houses have exposed beams beneath an upper floor, the floorboards are often an integral part of the ceiling below, in which case they cannot be lifted without consequent damage to the ceiling.

Parquet flooring

The blocks are often laid herringbone fashion and were a popular form of flooring in the early part of the twentieth century. The parquet blocks are usually up to about 25 mm thick and made of pitch pine or a hardwood and set in a bitumen-like compound. Missing pieces can be made up anew.

Tiled floors

These range from clay tiles, which were often square, through Victorian encaustic tiles (that have at least two or three different colours incorporated into them) to quarry tiles, which were also popular from Victorian times. Where original tiles remain, it is important to keep them and avoid trying to lift any of them as inevitably there will be breakages.

They were often covered over with another material when they went out of fashion. If they have been discovered under an impervious material, it may take many months for any dampness within or under the tiles to dry out. This may be visible as a grey bloom on the tiles which can be brushed off.

Do not use sealers on these types of floors as they can cause problems by trapping moisture in the tiles. It is also likely that the tiles may have been laid on a sub-floor where moisture was intended to evaporate out through the tile, rather than being sealed in.

Stone and brick floors

Where an original stone or brick floor exists avoid using sealants on them as this may cause problems to develop as any moisture that is already in the flooring or gets into it from whatever direction could be trapped and cause problems. Do not try to clean a natural floor with an abrasive cleaner as these can damage the surface and will remove the patina of age that is likely to have gathered.

The patina of age on this brick and stone floor is a valuable part of the appeal of the house.

Where re-pointing is necessary between the joints in the floor avoid using cement-based mortars or waterproof patent grouts as these trap moisture in the adjoining stone or brickwork and stop it from evaporating. A lime/sand mix may often be suitable.

Where a thin screed has in the past covered these floors, great care must be taken when trying to remove this so that the surface of the original material is not damaged. Where an existing floor has been covered over with another material it is likely that there was a reason for this rather than purely for fashion, so expect to find that repairs may be necessary to the underlying floor when re-exposed. Any floor coverings put on a natural floor should allow the underlying material to breathe, so avoid using foam-backed carpets or rugs.

Limeash, chalk and earth floors

Limeash floors, which were made using the by-products of lime-slaking, were often used for first floors, whereas chalk and earth floors are usually only found on the ground floor of a house. All these types of floors are primarily associated with particular parts of the country and are part of the local vernacular building tradition.

However, the things to avoid doing to them are similar. Do not use any proprietary sealants to cover them as this will alter their performance. Avoid using cement to repair any of these floors, instead try to find a supply of a similar material to the original to use for any repairs necessary.

Foam-backed carpets or any other covering that has an impervious backing to it should be avoided, as these will severely inhibit air circulation and may allow dampness to build up under the covering and degrade the floor.

Radiators and stoves

Where new means of heating an old house are to be introduced, think carefully about the visual impact that these could have. The design and location of radiators can detract from the setting of a room if not chosen with care. For example, when radiators are placed under windows they need to be lower than the cill so that the window details are not obscured.

When considering additions like solid fuel stoves they can have a strong visual impact on the room, which may not be as you intended. Choose your appliances with care.

Existing lighting

In an old house, using the existing locations for sockets and light fittings will avoid the damage that positioning new sockets and lighting points would cause. This may require a little ingenuity where problems need to be addressed like inconveniently placed light switches. Where walls have special features like wooden panelling, avoid cutting the panelling to receive a light switch. Either use a remote control or if necessary a surface-mounted switch.

Kitchens

The kitchen is the one room that is in constant use and so doing any work to this room is a major upheaval for the entire household. It may be better to do the kitchen last in the programme of work, so that you know exactly how much money you have left to spend on it and it does not get damaged by its inevitable use as a makeshift workshop and paintbrush cleaning station.

As many old houses have small kitchens, some people are very keen to open these up into breakfast rooms as well, although this is not practical in some houses. Whatever kitchen you inherit with an old house, it does form part of the house's history, so think about keeping that history.

Many older kitchen units were made entirely from solid timber, unlike most of their modern counterparts. Existing units can be adapted if you prefer or imaginatively refurbished, so that you have something that is truly unique. Purpose-built pantries are often removed when kitchens are re-designed, but it is actually very useful to have a walk-in cool storage area, as well as preserving part of the history and character of the house.

9

Surrounding an old house

An old house may have, where there is sufficient space around it, some outbuildings, hard landscape such as paths and drives, and soft landscape in the form of trees and plants.

Outbuildings

These create the setting around an old house and are an important part of the history of the house. Buildings or features constructed before 1 July 1948, which lie within the curtilage of a listed house, are usually also subject to listed building consent. Where alterations are proposed to outbuildings, or where a change of use is being proposed planning permission may also be necessary.

The quality of outbuildings usually reflects their secondary importance to the main house but many old houses have surprisingly sturdy and well-designed outbuildings. Whatever their quality, they are important as part of the setting and history of an old house and need to be treated with equal care and respect.

Outbuildings often use the local vernacular building traditions that may not be reflected in a grander house. For example, pantiles (the s-shaped red clay roof tiles) are often used on outbuildings when the main house has a more prestigious roof covering.

Regardless of the current use or lack of use, all old outbuildings need to be kept watertight in order to preserve them for future generations to enjoy and use. This is conservation in both current senses of the word, in that an existing historic building is retained and that new materials are not used up in creating a replacement building.

Privies were often the first buildings to be demolished when there was no longer a need for them. If you are lucky enough to still have one, look after it as they are diminishing in numbers.

Above – An old timber greenhouse in need of careful repair.

Don't allow ivy to take over an outbuilding.

Vegetation can change the emphasis of an elevation, unless kept under control.

Cart sheds were often converted into garages with the arrival of the motor car so these may give clues as to how they have evolved to accommodate later developments.

Very few traditional greenhouses survive as they were generally made of timber and tend to rot if not maintained on a regular basis. Old greenhouses can have wonderful old glass in them. If you do have an existing timber greenhouse, look after it and repair it. It will be impossible to replicate it exactly. It can only add interest, charm and value to an old house.

New outbuildings

Old houses are seen against the background of their setting. A good setting enhances an old house. So with individual houses or cottages, where new outbuildings like garages and stables are being considered, think about them in the same way that alteration or extensions might affect an old house. Old maps often show what outbuildings may have been demolished around an old house and may help you decide on the location of any new ancillary buildings.

New garages, where these are appropriate, need to be carefully sited in relation to an old house, as the bulk and size of a garage can visually dominate and overpower an old house. Any new outbuilding should not draw attention away from an old house. The roof pitch over a double garage can make the roof a dominant feature, if it is not designed in such a way as to reduce its bulk.

Clever use of local vernacular building detailing and materials together with a sympathetic location will help unite a new building with its existing surroundings and make it an attractive addition to the setting of an old house. Where an existing building has previously enjoyed space around it, this can be compromised if new buildings are sited so close so that it loses its dominance.

Work involving outbuildings and walls on boundaries

Listed building consent, for listed buildings, conservation area consent in conservation areas (for demolition) and planning permission may be required depending on the nature of the proposed work (see Chapter 2). Where walls or outbuildings form part of the wall or structure with adjoining neighbours they are classed as party walls. These and the Party Wall Act have been discussed earlier in Chapter 2.

Boundaries, drives and seating areas

How these elements are treated will have a very important effect on the setting for an old house. They can either dramatically enhance the house or do the complete opposite if they are not sensitively handled.

Before considering if anything needs doing look around to see which of these features still survive in the area as examples. You may be lucky to find someone in the row of cottages that hasn't knocked down their original front boundary wall, fence or hedge.

Where an old house forms part of a row of houses or cottages, the setting of the whole group of buildings can be badly damaged where front gardens are converted into car parking spaces. You have to decide whether what you have already is appropriate to the location and you can ask the local conservation officer for their input.Colours and textures are important. If you live in a country lane, then white painted ranch style fencing or a high brick boundary wall may not be appropriate to the setting. Use local materials as much as possible to continue the local vernacular tradition in the area. Where for example, dry stone walls already exist that have fallen down, these can be rebuilt re-using the existing materials.

Painted items such as fences take more effort to regularly maintain and will ultimately rot if not maintained. Alternatives may include hedges, walls or railings depending on the setting. Hedges need regular cutting but they can survive indefinitely and certainly longer than a fence. Stark walls are rather unfriendly as boundaries in the country and villages where hedges are the dominant boundary feature, so retain existing features that are in harmony with the surrounding area. Equally in towns, low front boundary walls, sometimes combined with hedges may be more appropriate to the character of a row of terraced houses.

There are many regional variations of walls depending on what was locally available. One area may have used locally available stone for walling, while in areas where flints and pebbles prevail, these are often incorporated into walls.

Brick and stone garden walls and how to care for them

While money is spent on the house, very little is often budgeted for repairing the walls and structures that surround it. When you have an old wall set in lime mortar, do not use a cement-based mortar for re-pointing, for the technical and aesthetic reasons explained earlier in this book. Where re-pointing is necessary, ensure that it matches the surrounding areas. Unsightly re-pointing to garden walls can only detract from the overall setting of an old house. The principles of repairs and re-pointing to old brick and stone walls are the same as for house walls (see Chapter 5).

Where ivy has been allowed to grow over an old wall it may be appropriate to remove it from time to time to limit damage to the wall. Try to avoid saplings getting established near walls as in time the tree or its roots may disturb the wall. Where soil has been piled high against an old wall, carefully remove this to allow air to circulate around the bricks again.

The life span of any type of old wall will be considerably increased if the top stones or copings are maintained, as these prevent water getting into the heart of the wall, preventing deterioration.

Brick and stone walls come in all shapes, styles, colours and sizes depending on the locally available materials. All brick walls have mortared joints whereas stone walls in certain areas are built without any mortar, these dry stone walls occur roughly north of a line drawn between Dorset and North Yorkshire. The bricks or stones used in garden walls may often be the left-overs from building the house, or in the case of dry stone walls, may have been found in the surrounding fields. A collapsed stone wall can usually be rebuilt with the original stones.

Enjoy dry stone walls, but don't let vegetation take over if it is likely to damage the wall.

Stone wall beginning to decay due to breakdown of weathered top.

Here a stone wall is a valuable part of the landscape and deserves careful maintenance.

Timber fences and gates

Old timber fences and gates are vulnerable to loss. Where fences and gates were painted the type of timber used and how regularly and how well they were painted determines their survival. Where they do still survive, they should be carefully repaired, with only the rotten pieces cut out and new pieces spliced in to the existing profile so that the maximum amount of original material is retained.

Any new timber fences or gates need to be appropriate to the local vernacular tradition, so look around your local neighbourhood to see what traditional vernacular detailing still exists, as certain styles of gates were once particular to different counties.

Avoid using fencing that is not particular to the area (DIY stores currently concentrate on a uniform range which rarely encompasses local variations). Choose new elements that are sensitive to local traditions.

Vertical slatted boarding, picket fencing or palings are often seen around old cottage gardens. Appropriate in some settings, possibly too informal for others. Fences are often seen together with hedges or plants, so think about how these would look together before making any decisions.

Metal gates and railings

Metal gates and railings were made from one of two very different materials and the distinction is usually evident by the design. Wrought iron is a malleable iron heated up and hammered into shape, capable of fine details. The joints can grow out of the iron or be assembled in a way similar to carpentry joints. Cast iron (which is a more brittle material) is moulded into pre-determined shapes that are difficult to adjust once cast, so designs are based upon the repetition of standard elements, often bolted together.

Welded and bent steel is often sold as wrought iron (because technically at least it is iron which has been wrought) but owes little to the real traditions of the blacksmith. The difference is that it is made from uniform standard round, square, flat or tubular sections with knobbly welded joints. Today most new metal gates are usually made from mild steel, even though the details may be based on those used in wrought ironwork.

New cast iron and real wrought iron railings and gates can be made to appropriate designs for a great variety of situations. New real wrought iron is still comparatively rare today. It is a crafts-based product but it is making a healthy comeback. Cast iron has never really gone away from mainstream building. It has been relegated to products like high quality rainwater goods and manhole covers but has never entirely been superseded by steel and plastic.

Metal railings may either be used alone or in combination with other materials like a brick or stone wall plinth on which they sit. Sometimes you might get a clue about where railings have been removed. If you see square pieces of metal set into a stone or render coping at regular intervals, this usually indicates that the railings have been cut off. This happened particularly during the 1939–1945 war where railings were removed with the idea of contributing to the war effort.

Gates and railings can have a substantial impact on the setting of the house, so it is vitally important to choose new gates and railings, where none exist, that complement rather than compete with an old house. Look at old photographs of your area to see what types of railing were used and what examples still survive.

From a practical point of view, gates may have to admit a range of vehicles as well as visitors on foot. Make sure that railings and gates are

Existing entrance gates and walls help define houses, especially formal ones where they should be carefully preserved.

regularly painted and keep a look out for signs of rust and deal with them before they get a hold. It is also possible to get repairs carried out, providing you find someone who understands the metals involved. Cast iron for example is very brittle and likely to crack if heated carelessly.

There are now metal primers and undercoats available that are designed for use in protecting metal in very exposed situations (oilrigs, ships) and using these properly will ensure a much longer-term protection from rust. They tend to be thicker coatings so avoid using if you have very finely detailed work to show off.

Left – Cast iron fencing.

Below – Simple wrought iron fencing.

Hedges and ditches

Hedges can add a great deal to the setting of an old house, providing that appropriate (and often native) species are used that are in keeping with the immediate setting of the house and the wider locality. In hedges that are more formal these tend to be yew, beech, holly and privet, while a mixture of hedgerow species are more usual in informal hedges.

There is legislation under the Hedgerows Regulations 1997, which protects rural field boundaries and consent for their removal is required from the local council. There are variations to these regulations, in respect of a domestic curtilage. Contact the arboricultural officer at your local council who should be able to advise you.

When planting new hedges, give careful thought to how high the hedge could grow in future and whether the roots of a tall hedge could affect any adjoining buildings. Many types of hedges can easily obscure a delightful elevation if allowed to grow too tall. Ditches are a useful refuge for wildlife both in towns and the country, so maintain them but allow them to develop naturally rather than trying to over tidy or change them where this is not appropriate to the immediate setting. Consent from the Environment Agency may be required if any filling in or piping of a ditch or watercourse is proposed.

Hard landscape

This term is used to refer to the materials that surround an old house like drives and pathways. It is advisable to avoid using any man-made products as they are made to very precise dimensions, colours and texture ranges. Paving stones which are too regular and do not weather in the same way as natural materials may appear intrusive and inappropriate in traditional settings. Old houses and their surroundings are by contrast made from natural materials that were inherently variable and often irregular.

It is sensible to avoid putting impervious materials immediately adjacent to old walls as their presence will prevent moisture escaping from the ground as explained when dealing with dampness (see Chapter 4).

Where a recent concrete path has been laid abutting the wall of an old house, it is wise to try to remove at least a 300 mm wide section of the path against a house so that the house walls can breathe again. Perhaps this may further benefit from the addition of a French drain.

Pleasing textures make an old house appealing – hedges can hide architectural details if allowed to grow too tall.

There are many varieties of naturally available materials to set off an old house, such as stone, bricks and cobbles, use locally available materials where possible. Creating a subtle environment is about getting the right balance and not overdoing the setting so that an old house has to compete with it. A cottage is unlikely to look right if the hard landscape is paved similar to an out-of-town supermarket car park.

Seating areas are often sited close to the existing house which is the backdrop. Breaking up the paving into smaller areas of different materials and using planting to soften may be appropriate. Gravel or stone chippings are adaptable, cheap and drain freely so can be laid close to the house wall.

Timber decks are currently popular but they are an import from a different climate. Time will tell whether carpeting the garden with wood is a good idea in damp Britain and it will certainly be a test for wood treatments and stains. Using local managed timber is better in global conservation terms.

Where existing paths or seating areas have been created using concrete, they do weather with age, but you may decide that you would like to add a natural surface to disguise them and break the surface up visually by using gravel, planting, bricks or even mosaic inserts. Be careful not to build up the levels against the walls of the house.

Exterior lighting

Carefully chosen light fittings can enhance an old house at night, while unsympathetic and inappropriate ones can distract the eye from the overall harmony of an old house by day and night. Exterior lighting, as with interior lighting, is about creating a subtle setting. Too much illumination is more likely to spoil an old house if badly done. Also, be careful about light pollution as poorly positioned light fittings may shine directly at neighbours or passing road or pavement users.

Consider how you can reduce the energy consumption of external lighting by using low-energy bulbs and having lights on timers or activated by remote control.

As the ability to illuminate external areas permanently is relatively new, there is less historical precedent for external lighting of many types of domestic properties. Reproduction street-lamps are an urban feature, which look out of place at a cottage, so choose light fittings that are suited to the situation. Aesthetically, it would seem best to light paths with discreet low-level garden lighting and supplement this with a fitting at the door for convenience and security. Security lighting can be combined with these and can often be triggered by sensors rather than the lamps always being illuminated.

Left – These gardens are the perfect setting for well-maintained cottages.

Below – Traditional building forms have existed for so long that they have become an accepted part of the landscape.

10

Trees and gardens

Trees and gardens can take a long time to mature in contrast to building works that are relatively immediate. Usually an old house is tackled first and only then is attention turned to a possibly mature but neglected garden. It does take time for a neglected garden to grow back into shape, especially after being a building site.

A sensible approach is to start developing the garden in tandem with the house, so that new plants have time to grow, while any overgrown plants that have to be pruned have time to recover.

Where works are being carried out to an old house, an area around it will be necessary for access and storage of building materials and care should be taken to choose the least sensitive areas to store these materials.

Trees and their legal protection

Trees can be protected in one of two ways when associated with old houses.

Individual trees, groups of trees or woodlands can be subject to specific legal protection known as tree preservation orders (TPOs).

Trees in conservation areas are also protected where the trunk diameter is 75 mm or greater at a height of 1.5 metres above ground level. There are certain exceptions for commercial forestry and some fruit trees. An application for work to a tree in a conservation area, which is made to the tree or arboricultural officer at the local council, may takes six weeks, while a tree subject to a tree preservation order may take eight weeks.

Carrying out works to protected trees

Contact the tree or arboricultural officer at the local council to discuss any work you would like to carry out to a protected tree before making an application. They may be able to advise you on what is acceptable, and what work will suit the location, before an application is made to the local council. An application for work that is likely to enhance the life-span of a tree is usually looked on favourably.

Where old trees are experiencing problems, there are often several alternatives as to how to deal with the problem and still keep the tree, so if you are unhappy with the advice that you have been given by a tree surgeon or anyone else, because it seems an insensitive solution, always obtain a second opinion.

A written application has to be made to a local council, either on a form supplied by them or by a written letter covering all the appropriate details about the works together with the location of the tree and reasons for the work. There is currently no fee attached to this type of application.

Trees and building works

Where building works are being carried out near trees, they need to be protected in accordance with *British Standard BS 5837: Guide for Trees in Relation to Construction* (1991). This includes protecting tree trunks and the root zone from physical damage and protecting the tree canopy from damage by vehicles and machinery by the siting of protective fencing at the edge of the tree canopy. This will also protect the tree roots from compaction of the soil by vehicles as this can damage the ability of tree roots to function.

A tree may never fully recover from damage if injured boughs and roots allow disease and rot to get established. As most tree roots are generally within 600 mm of the surface, it is important to ensure that chemicals are not allowed to leak into the soil and poison the roots.

Avoid siting trenches close to trees, as cutting tree roots will affect the supply of water and nutrients to a tree and could reduce the stability of the tree. It is likely that the radius of a tree's root system can extend horizontally to a distance equivalent to its height, so be careful about what activities take place near any trees.

Trees and their proximity to old houses

There has been a lot of debate about trees being allowed to grow too close to houses.

Trees can obscure both attractive and unattractive buildings, but remember this can change with the seasons.

There are cases where trees do cause problems but in many instances problems are perceived rather than real and more to do with inconvenience than danger. Avoid any future problems by planting new trees well away from old houses. This is sensible as a tree can often obscure a substantial part of an elevation when planted too close. Self-set saplings should be discouraged from taking root too close to an old house, walls or outbuildings, so move them before they get too big. Many trees started out as saplings at the back of a flowerbed and then were overlooked.

Trees, neighbours and new owners

Most people turn their attention to trees when they first move into a house. Remember that local authority permissions may be necessary before any work starts.

It takes time to get to know a garden through all the seasons, so allow plenty of time to come to decisions about trees. The situation is irreversible once trees have been cut down.

Trees on boundaries with adjoining neighbours can be contentious, usually because one party wants exactly the opposite of the other. For example neighbours often cite tree roots as potential dangers, when in reality the problem is too much shade being cast by the tree. Enjoy trees for what they are – sculptural additions to the surroundings that reflect the changing seasons and help the environment provide the air we breathe.

Having pleaded for the survival of trees there comes a time when every tree is too frail to safely be left. This is not necessarily when the inside of the trunk becomes hollow, as that is part of the natural cycle of a growing tree designed to keep it stable. Trees need to be inspected by knowledgeable people and an assessment made on facts rather than fears.

Finding the right person to prune the trees

From time to time trees may need to be pruned and it is vitally important to find a tree surgeon that is sensitive as well as artistic. They need to also be experienced in their approach to the particular types of trees that need pruning. A lot of tree work often involves felling rather than pruning, make sure that where pruning is involved that you find someone who is good at that.

The tree officer at the local council will usually be able to give you some suggestions for suitably qualified tree surgeons, but also ask friends and relatives and the Arboricultural Association for suggestions. Make sure that the people you engage to work on trees carry adequate insurance as mistakes and accidents with trees have the potential to be quite dramatic. Tree surgeons should operate in accordance with best practice and *British Standard BS 3998: Recommendations for Tree Work* (1989).

Archaeology

If you think there may be something of archaeological interest in your garden and you would like to find out more about it speak to the archaeology unit at your county council. Keep an eye on lawns in dry weather for signs of dissimilar areas showing through from the subsoil.

Gardens

Before doing anything to the garden take record photographs as these are useful for future reference. A garden will look very different during the seasons, so capture as many of the changes as possible. Take stock of the existing features in the garden, and identify the existing plants and trees that combine to make it an interesting place.

Where to go for help with the garden

There is a range of professionals who can help you with the garden, from landscape architects and garden designers to pool, pond and wildflower meadow specialists. Who you go to depends on what you want to achieve and your budget. Landscape architects and garden designers will both be able to create a design for the garden, but whereas landscape architects are trained in all areas of landscape design, garden designers are more focused on gardens. Ideally any new design for an old garden would try to incorporate the existing attractive or historic features rather than starting afresh.

Creating a garden yourself

As with discovering the history of an old house, information about the garden may also be uncovered. Old large-scale maps may give an indication of what buildings have been demolished in a garden. Local people who have known the area for a long time may also be able to help.

Where trees are planted in such a way that they do not relate to the existing house, or where garden walls are at an odd angle to the house, this may indicate that they related to other buildings. If there are lumps in the lawn, these could signal the remains of old outbuildings or garden features.

Make sure you know exactly what plants, hedges and trees you have before you proceed, as it is unusual for an old house not to have established trees and shrubs of some sort already. Changes, once made to a garden, can often be slow to reverse. Think what the effect will be on the setting for an old house and whether these changes enhance that or not. Pruning a tree or some ivy may bring you face to face with something that you would rather not see from the house. Dense trees and vegetation can also help mask noise.

Extending the garden

Sometimes the opportunity may arise to purchase a piece of adjoining land to enlarge the garden. If you are purchasing farmland for use as a garden, you may be required to apply to the local council for planning permission for change of use.

Ponds and lakes

Old maps or historical records may indicate where such features existed in the past, which may give an indication as to where to look in the garden for evidence. Where there is space for large expanses of water to be created as either ponds or lakes, planning permission may be necessary depending on the proposed size.

Trees and gardens help to frame old houses.

11

Conclusions

I f you can enjoy the patina of age and the imperfections and occasional inconveniences that are part of the character of old
houses, without being upset by the door that occasionally sticks,
or the beam that is that little bit too low, then you may be compatible
with living in an old house.

It is all too easy to unwittingly destroy the subtle visual qualities of
an old house by bland redecoration and unnecessary straightening. It is
equally easy to innocently engender decay by introducing inappropriate
modern materials.

Living in an old house is partly about enjoying a certain level of
pleasing decay, without immediately rushing out and replacing it. It is
the pleasure of a genuine antique rather than a reproduction. The skill
of living in and enjoying an old house is to be relaxed about its short-
comings but it is also about knowing when the time really has come for
a little careful repair.

I hope this book will have enabled you to be more confident and
secure in the understanding of old houses and their surroundings so
that you are more able to live in harmony with each other.

The author may be contacted through the website www.oldhouse.info.

Living in old houses is about enjoying them as they are. A worn stone step records the number of feet that have passed over the threshold. Renewing it would erase history.

Appendix

In order to gain a greater understanding about the properties of lime, the following is an explanation as to why lime is so good for old buildings.

What is lime?

The product that is used on old buildings has to go through a number of processes from its natural state before it can be used. This starts with lumps of quarried limestone (calcium carbonate) being burnt at about 900°C. The resulting 'quick lime' (calcium oxide) is then mixed with water, which creates a violent chemical reaction. The water becomes hot and bubbles furiously as the quick lime dissolves in the water. This process is called 'slaking'.

When all the lime has dissolved the reaction stops and the solution will then start to cool down. It will by now begin to look like thick yoghurt and is called lime putty (calcium hydroxide). Few people have seen lime putty before becoming associated with old buildings. However they may have seen it in its hydrated form as sold in garden centres for increasing the alkalinity of garden soil. This is a fine white powder and is made by slaking the 'quick lime' with less water, so that a powder is created at the end rather than the liquid or paste of lime putty. This powder is called 'bag lime' or hydrated lime and is, arguably, to lime putty what dried milk is to bottled milk. When mixed with water it makes a passable version of the 'real' product.

When the lime putty is exposed to the air, over a period of time it carbonates and turns into calcium carbonate as it hardens.

Perhaps the major downside of lime is that it is a caustic substance and gloves and goggles must be worn when using it in all its various forms.

Lime is now gaining conservation credentials, in the wider meaning of the word, as it is now being suggested that during the drying process it absorbs the equivalent carbon to that released in the initial burning process.

When applying limewash wear goggles and rubber gloves as lime is a caustic substance. Make sure you mix enough pigmented limewash for each elevation as it is very difficult to colour match different batches.

Cement is processed at higher temperatures (1300 to 1500°C as opposed to around 900°C for lime) and involves other materials as well as limestone. It can also act as a 'carbon sink' when curing into concrete. It will be interesting to watch how these relative qualities are researched and exploited in our carbon-conscious future.

It is worth mentioning that cement can set without exposure to air, where lime only hardens on exposure to air. One of cement's applications was in the building of lighthouses because it could cure under water, in the absence of air.

Lime (non-hydraulic lime) can take a very long time to harden if laid too thick or if trapped deep inside a structure. It is conceivable, and sometimes claimed, that pockets of unset lime exist inside thick walls of old buildings after many years. That would be exceptional but it highlights one of lime's other strengths – that it can adapt to movement by apparently disintegrating and then re-setting itself. Of course it does not re-trace the precise chemical processes of its original manufacture – but it acts as if it does. This is why old brick or stone walls can slowly move over the years without showing any cracks.

Some limes, called hydraulic limes, set in a similar way to cement in the absence of air. There are presently concerns that some of the unwanted properties of cement can also come with this, like excessive strength after a certain period of time for example.

Lime – a summary of the types

At this point it is probably helpful to give a resumé of the types of lime introduced above as unhelpfully most of them sound very similar:

Lime putty (also called non-hydraulic lime)
A thick white yoghurt-looking lime used in building, purchased 'ready-made' in plastic tubs and often specified to be 'matured' (that is, it is thought best not to use it too fresh). This is available from specialist suppliers throughout the country usually in plastic airtight containers.

Hydrated lime (also called 'bag lime')
A white powder available at most builders' merchants in paper sacks. When mixed with water (wear goggles and gloves) it reproduces lime putty and can be used like for like, though some regard it as second-rate. Be careful that the bags have been stored absolutely dry or you will be buying a bag of useless chalk.

Hydrated lime must be mixed with clean water prior use. A minimum should be 48 hours but the longer that it is left to absorb the water the better. If stored in an airtight container it can be kept for many months.

Hydraulic lime
Also in powder form, this sets by a reaction when mixed rather than just on exposure to air (hence 'hydraulic' because they were supposed to set even under water). Pure hydraulic limes are available in various grades (quaintly known by names such as feebly hydraulic, moderately hydraulic and eminently hydraulic) as well as modern commercially mass-produced versions – sometimes with admixtures to emulate such traditional gradings.

There is a European classification for the strengths of modern hydraulic limes. Most hydraulic limes are produced outside the United Kingdom. Responses are mixed with some fears that they are too hard to replace non-hydraulic lime putty. Nevertheless a more predictable product is promised, to sit alongside lime putty, which can be used in areas where a more durable mortar is needed without resorting to cement.

The European classifications for natural hydraulic limes are NHL 2, 3.5 and 5, which indicate the minimum strength achieved after 28 days ranging from weaker to stronger.

Cement (Portland cement)

Because it has some unsympathetic properties and can so easily be mis-used on old buildings it is best kept well away from historic fabric unless there are compelling reasons. Until recently, 'weak' cement/lime mixes were in widespread use in conservation but as confidence has grown in the re-discovery of lime skills, cement has slowly been abandoned.

Cement has unequalled structural possibilities when used in rein-forced concrete and this perhaps helped it into universal use in more modest projects. It does behave very predictably and it is suitable for adaptation to today's mechanised building processes.

Neither lime nor cement can be used in very cold conditions because the high water content in the mix can freeze before the product hardens and permanently derange it. However cement can be laid shortly before the winter in the knowledge that it should have reached a certain strength in a known number of days, whereas lime can remain un-set for an unpredictably long time so it is best used only in the spring and summer.

Chemical admixtures can be used to protect cement from freezing but this is not considered appropriate for lime because it is thought to impede the setting action.

It has only been in the last decades that it has begun to be under-stood exactly how much damage old buildings can suffer from the use of cement. Amongst conservation professionals the tide has now turned back in favour of lime-based products for use on old buildings.

White cement

White cement is supposed to look like lime when set and is often thrown into cement mixes to fake a lime appearance, but it is cement not lime.

Pozzolanic additives

There are additives that can be put into non-hydraulic lime to make it set in a broadly similar way to that achieved by hydraulic limes. They range from crushed brick dust (specially fired) to PFA (pulverised fuel ash) and HTI (high temperature insulation). These materials vary quite widely in their qualities and should be used under expert guidance.

It is probable that these additives may reduce the porosity and permeability of the mortar slightly, they are usually dark colours so this may affect the overall colour of the mortar.

If a pozzolanic additive is to be included in a mortar mix this should be done just before the mortar is to be used and limited to a small proportion of the mix.

Accidental ingredient?

Possibly there is another variety of 'pozzolanic' type set of lime putty which could be a traditional but accidental ingredient that got into the mix from the earth sides of the lime pit dug on each old building site. Our post-cement clinical treatment of lime has lacked this rustic ingredient which, it is thought, might have possibly contributed to the longevity of some historic lime mortars and renders: natural clay.

Another angle from which to consider traditional 'additives' is the logistics of transport. When it took a day to get to the nearest supplier of materials, they were probably more likely to 'make do' with anything that was found in the immediate surroundings. So 'dirty' sand was likely to be used in mixes and this dirt may similarly have contributed to the mix.

What is lime used for in old buildings?

Lime has two very useful properties: it is permeable and it is slightly flexible. It is also a versatile material and can be used in the following materials for old houses:

- Mortar mixes and grouts
- External renders and internal plasters
- Limewash paint finish, both externally and internally
- Limeash floors

Mortar mixes

Non-hydraulic lime mortar is slightly softer than traditional soft red bricks, or some building stones. This makes them ideal partners. The lime degrades first. That is acceptable as this 'sacrificial' element can be replaced by re-pointing, which may only happen every century or so. If the soft bricks or stones were to degrade first (which they would if they had been set in cement mortar) then the problems are far greater. You cannot after all replace the bricks or stones and leave the mortar. The perfect balance in any traditional brickwork or stonework is that the mortar is slightly softer than the bricks or stones.

A useful by-product of a soft lime mortar is that it is possible to clean it off the bricks or stones and re-use them. That is very rarely possible with cement mortar.

The general convention is that a good starting point for a mortar mix for old buildings is 3 parts of sand to 1 part of lime. However, there are a great many variations to this mix. To put this in the context of current day thinking; most builders' standard mortar mix is also a 3:1 mix, but of 3 parts sand to 1 part cement. This is a very much harder and less flexible mix than lime.

Using and mixing lime-based materials takes a lot of experience to know how to use them appropriately – it is not too fanciful to compare the use of lime to learning any other craft.

Inexperience in using lime-based products can lead to it not having hardened sufficiently before winter frosts, these can damage lime mortars if not sufficiently hardened and so it gets an undeserved bad name.

Lime is only really usable between May and October each year in England and between June and September, with careful use, in Scotland. It is preferable to use it earlier in the season, so that it has all the summer to harden. How quickly this happens will be dependent on location and weather, which if poor can mean that the lime is unable to harden sufficiently before winter frosts.

Frost damage is usually identifiable by a crumbling outer surface of say a mortar used for re-pointing. It is more likely to become apparent in exposed situations where lime mortar is used around ridge tiles, on roofs or for re-pointing on chimneys. In these localised exposed situations, it may be advisable to add a setting ingredient to these mortar mixes. The options are usually hydraulic lime or a pozzolanic additive. Each of these ingredients can help speed up the set of the mortar, but equally they can also reduce the desirable natural qualities of a non-hydraulic lime mortar.

There is debate at present about the use of hydraulic limes and cement in lime mortar mixes. It is known that hydraulic limes can double in strength over an 18-month period. This can mean that they end up being stronger than a non-hydraulic lime plus cement mix.

Builders carrying out work involving lime mixes may, if they feel inexperienced in the use of lime mortars, be tempted to add cement or hydraulic lime if it is available to make sure the mortar sets in a way that they are familiar with. This would result in a mortar which can be expected to incorporate the worst features of all ingredients.

External renders and internal plasters

In Scotland external renders are called 'harling' while south of the border they are usually called renders or lime renders. Internal work is called both render and plaster (not to be confused with 'real' plaster of Paris or gypsum plaster).

These are again used in generally similar proportions to mortar mixes, of 3 parts sand to 1 part lime for both renders and plaster. It is usual for three coats of plaster to be applied, with each coat getting thinner. The proportions also usually differ slightly between coats, with the weakest coat as the topcoat. Hair may be added to the undercoats to reinforce it and to help reduce shrinkage cracks when drying.

The topcoat may use finer sand to give a smoother finish and the lime will be worked to the surface by the plasterer again to give a smoother finish. While a 3 parts sand to 1 part lime mix is a good starting point, variations can be many and varied depending of the availability of local materials and local craftspeople's own preferences and experience.

Why are lime renders and plasters good for old buildings?

When used in renders and plasters, lime's slight flexibility helps an old building in several ways. Renders and plasters are usually applied direct to brick, stone or onto timber laths. (These are horizontal timber strips, fixed to timber supporting studs or joists so that render or plaster can be applied to the laths, by squeezing the mix through the gaps between the strips to form a securing key for the render or plaster, so that it doesn't drop off. This technique is basically the same for both walls and ceilings).

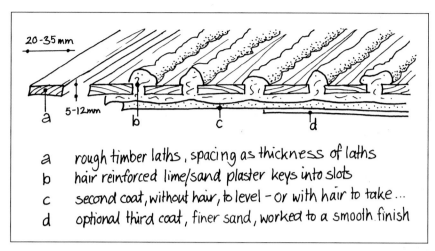

20-35 mm

5-12mm

a

b

c

d

a   rough timber laths, spacing as thickness of laths
b   hair reinforced lime/sand plaster keys into slots
c   second coat, without hair, to level – or with hair to take...
d   optional third coat, finer sand, worked to a smooth finish

An example of how lath and plaster works.

Renders and plasters are applied to substrates which are susceptible to movement in old buildings. This is because the bricks, stones or timbers used expand and contract slightly due to thermal expansion as a result of seasonal variations, and possibly the level of heating within the house. Many old houses were built on rudimentary foundations which may also move slightly.

If the background that the render or plaster is applied to is likely to move slightly then it follows that there is usually some mobility in the render or plaster finish, so that cracks, which will let water in if the render is external, are avoided.

Lime-based plasters and renders are also usefully breathable so that any moisture that gets into a house is allowed to escape through these materials.

And cement and modern internal plasters?

Given that old buildings are susceptible to movement and lime renders can tolerate this then lime is the preferred material. Ordinary cement renders are more brittle than lime and once they crack and let water in the dampness cannot evaporate so readily through cement render.

Internally the modern version of lime rendering (or plastering) is a gypsum-based product. This is usually a pinky-red in colour. As with cement these materials have been developed to suit the modern building industry and produce a very fine surface predictably and quickly. But where lime can tolerate dampness passing through it in small doses, some gypsum plasters can become saturated very quickly because the material likes to incorporate moisture into itself.

Gypsum, in the form of plaster of Paris, has been added into fine plasterwork historically – but only in areas free from dampness. It does permit a much finer surface, almost like glass, to be worked up.

In the right conditions modern gypsum plasters are excellent materials. But if the walls are bent and bowed and the ceilings comfortably sagging then does a plaster that approaches the sharpness of glass seem appropriate or would the softer texture of lime plaster be more fitting?

Limewash

Diluting lime putty with water makes limewash. A typical mix of one part lime putty to one and a half or two parts water is a good rule of thumb. As with all natural materials it is a matter of trying this to see how well it works and then adjusting the mix to suit the porosity of the surface. Remember that the wall surface needs to be thoroughly wetted with water prior to applying the limewash, so that the water is not instantly sucked out of the newly applied limewash. Also it takes several hours (or days) for the limewash to dry and for the true colour to become apparent.

As a general principle the less you add to a limewash in terms of pigments the better, a rule of thumb is a maximum of 10%.

Limewash is usually applied over external lime-based renders. It can be used internally for walls and ceilings, but as it is likely to brush off when touched, a natural binder can be incorporated, however that does make it less permeable.

It is vitally important to use eye protection when applying limewash. Contact of lime with any part of the body should be avoided until the product is set, when it becomes relatively harmless.

Why is limewash good for old buildings?

Limewash is compatible with lime renders, lime mortars, brickwork, stone and timber (it clings better on rough timber).

It is, like lime render, vapour permeable and will automatically fill small cracks in lime render and help 'heal' them.

Unlike most modern paints it weathers by slowly eroding away – so it does not crack and cannot hold reservoirs of water against the wall. This also makes preparation for re-decoration easier.

Logically, as limewash is a caustic application, it must help sterilise the surface though it cannot be relied upon to kill all algae and these can be removed first with compatible methods. Limewash's random colour variations (with application and weathering) will soften and add character to a building, in contrast to the uniformity of modern paints.

And modern paints?

Modern paints, masonry paints based on plastics and resins, and timber gloss paints based on oil and solvents, tend to try to form a skin on the surface of the wall. They are uniform in appearance and, like other industrial products, are expected to do a certain job in a predictable way on a predictable surface.

Most modern masonry paints are designed for use on modern buildings which are themselves designed not to move and are carefully detailed to shed water. Applied over lime render these 'plastic' paints tend to help trap leaks and condensation inside the fabric. Their precise colour finish is also arguably counter-productive and bland when finishing an otherwise pleasantly imprecise old building.

Modern paints might be acceptable to be used on old buildings if the structure didn't need to breathe and didn't move, but when they do move the paint film begins to crack and let water through. Because these paints are generally not very breathable they do not allow this water to dry out again sufficiently fast.

Further reading

House Research

Barratt, Nick, *Tracing the History of the House*, Public Record Office, 2001

House Type History

Brunskill, R.W., *Illustrated Handbook of Vernacular Architecture*,
Faber & Faber, London, 1970

Brunskill, R.W., *Brick Building in Britain*, Victor Gollancz, London, 1997

Brunskill, R.W., *Houses and Cottages of Britain*, Victor Gollancz,
London, 1997

Brunskill, R.W., *Timber-Framed Building in Britain*, Victor Gollancz,
London, 1999

Clifton-Taylor, Alec, *The Pattern of English Building*, Faber & Faber,
London, 1972

Curl, James Stevens, *Encyclopaedia of Architectural Terms*, Donhead,
Shaftesbury, 1997

Harris, Richard, *Timber-Framed Buildings*, Shire Publications,
Princes Risborough, 3rd Edition, 1993

Innocent, C.F., *The Development of English Building Construction*,
(1916 Edition), Donhead, Shaftesbury, 1999

Iredale, David and Barrett, John, *Discovering Your Old House*,
Shire Publications, Princes Risborough, 3rd Edition, 1991

London Terrace Houses: 1660–1860, English Heritage, London, 1996

Loudon, John Claudius, *Encyclopaedia of Cottage, Farm, and Villa
Architecture and Furniture*, (1833 Edition), Volumes 1 and 2, Donhead,
Shaftesbury, 2000

Muthesius, Stefan, *The English Terraced House*, Yale University Press, 1982,
4th printing, New Haven and London, 1990

Powell, Christopher, *Discovering Cottage Architecture*, Shire Publications,
Princes Risborough, reprinted 1996

Pevsner, Nikolaus et al, *The Buildings of England, Ireland, Wales and Scotland*,
Penguin, London, for each county

Interiors – General

Bristow, Ian C, *Architectural Colour in British Interiors 1615–1840*,
    Yale University Press, New Haven and London, 1996
Bristow, Ian C, *Interior House-Painting Colours and Technology 1615–1840*,
    Yale University Press, New Haven and London, 1996
Calloway, Stephen and Jones, Stephen, *Traditional Style, How to Recreate the
    Traditional Period Home*, Pyramid Books, London, 1990
Lander, Hugh and Rauter, Peter, *English Cottage Interiors*, Cassell & Co,
    London, 2001

Mediaeval Houses

Wood, Margaret, *The English Mediaeval House*, Ferndale Editions,
    London, 1981

Georgian Houses

The Georgian Group publishes advisory leaflets on the following subjects:
    1 Windows; 2 Brickwork; 3 Doors; 4 Paint Colour; 5 Render, Stucco and
    Plaster; 6 Wallpaper; 7 Mouldings; 8 Ironwork; 9 Fireplaces; 10 Roofs;
    11 Floors; 12 Stonework; 13 Lighting; 14 Curtains and Blinds
    15 Papier-mâché.
Cranfield, Ingrid, *Georgian House Style, An Architectural and Interior Design
    Source Book*, David & Charles, Newton Abbot, 2001
Parissien, Steven, *The Georgian Group Book of The Georgian House*,
    Aurum Press, London, 1995

Victorian Houses

The Victorian Society publish advisory leaflets on the following subjects:
    1. Doors; 2. Decorative Tiles; 3 Fireplaces; 4 Interior Mouldings;
    5 Wallcoverings; 6 Cast iron; 7 brickwork; 8 Paintwork; 9 Timber
    Windows
Johnson, Alan, *How to Restore and Improve your Victorian House*,
    David & Charles, Newton Abbot, 1991
Long, Helen, *Victorian Houses and their Details*, Butterworth-Heinemann,
    Oxford, 2001
Osband, Linda, *Victorian House Style, An Architectural and Interior Design
    Source Book*, David & Charles, Newton Abbot, 2001
Osband, Linda, *Victorian Gothic House Style, An Architectural and Interior
    Design Source Book*, David & Charles, Newton Abbot, 2001
Wedd, Kit, *The Victorian Society Book of The Victorian House*, Aurum Press,
    London, 2002

Arts and Crafts

Kelley, Charlotte, *The Arts and Crafts Source Book*, Thames and Hudson, London, 2001

Edwardian Houses

Hockman, Hilary, *Edwardian House Style, An Architectural and Interior Design Source Book*, David & Charles, Newton Abbot, 2001

Long, Helen C, *The Middle-Class Home in Britain 1880–1914*, Manchester University Press, Manchester, 1993

Art Deco

Cranfield, Ingrid, *Art Deco House Style, An Architectural and Interior Design Source Book*, David & Charles, Newton Abbot, 2001

Interiors – Specific Items

Eastop, Dinah and Gill, Kathryn, *Upholstery Conservation: Principles and Practice*, Butterworth-Heinemann, Oxford, 2000

Eveleigh, David, *Firegrates and Kitchen Ranges*, Shire Publications, Princes Risborough, 1990

Gledhill, David, *Gas Lighting*, Shire Publications, Princes Risborough, 1987

Guidelines for the Conservation of Textiles, English Heritage, London, 1996

Meadows, Cecil A., *Discovering Oil Lamps*, Shire Publications, Princes Risborough, 1992

Miller, Judith, *Period Details: A Source Book for House Restoration*, Mitchell Beazley, London, 1987

Sandwith, Hermione and Stainton, Sheila, *The National Trust Manual of Housekeeping*, Penguin, London, 1984

Legal

Mynors, Charles, *Listed Buildings, Conservation Areas and Monuments*, 3rd Edition, Sweet & Maxwell, London, 1999

Historical Building Control and Grants, Technical Pamphlet G2, SPAB, London, 1984

VAT

VAT and Historic Buildings, Technical Pamphlet G1, SPAB, London. The following are available from HM Customs and Excise and on their website:

VAT information sheet 4/01: VAT Budget Changes: Vat reduced rates – urban regeneration measures

VAT information sheet 8/01: VAT Budget Changes: Adjustments to the zero rate for sale of renovated properties

Notice 708: Buildings and construction

Notice 719: VAT refunds for 'do-it-yourself' builders and converters

Building Materials in General
Emerton, Gerald, *The Pattern of Scottish Roofing*, Research Report,
    Historic Scotland, Edinburgh, 2000
Wright, Adela, *Craft Techniques for Traditional Buildings*, B.T. Batsford,
    London, 1991

Practical and Technical Advice
Leaflets are available from the following:
Society for the Protection of Ancient Buildings – www.spab.org.uk
Georgian Group – www.georgiangroup.org.uk
Victorian Society – www.victorian-society.org.uk
English Heritage – www.english-heritage.org.uk
Historic Scotland – www.historic-scotland.gov.uk
Environment and Heritage Service – Northern Ireland – www.ehsni.gov.uk
The Dry Stone Walling Association of Great Britain – www.dswa.org.uk

Local Authority Advice Guides
Many local authorities produce very good free guides, other publications can
be purchased. A couple are suggested below:
Historic Buildings: Repairs, Alterations and Extensions, Suffolk Coastal District
    Council, August 1997
Essex County Council produces a number of guides on various subjects

Advice Guides
*The West End Conservation Manual, A Guide to the Maintenance, Repair and
    Conservation of Victorian and Edwardian Buildings in Glasgow's West End*,
    1999
Davey, Heath, Hodges, *The Care and Conservation of Georgian Buildings*,
    Edinburgh New Town Conservation Committee, 4th Edition, 1995
Joyce, Barry, *Derbyshire – Detail and Character*, Sutton Publishing,
    Stroud, 1996

Advice on Repairs
Brereton C., *The Repair of Historic Buildings: Advice on Principles and
    Methods*, English Heritage, London, 2nd Edition, 1995
Lander, Hugh, *House and Cottage Restoration, Dos & Don'ts*, Acanthus Books,
    Redruth, 1999
Lander, Hugh, *The House Restorer's Guide*, David & Charles,
    Newton Abbot, 1986
The Repair of Historic Buildings in Scotland, Advice on Principles and Methods
    edited by John Knight, Historic Scotland, Edinburgh, 1995

Powys, A.R., *Repair of Ancient Buildings*, The Society for the Protection of
Ancient Buildings, reprinted 1981

Robson, Patrick, *Structural Repair of Traditional Buildings*, Donhead,
Shaftesbury, 1999

Specific Building Materials and Problems

Ashurst, John and Nicola, Practical Building Conservation Series, English
Heritage Technical Handbooks, Gower Technical Press, Aldershot, 1988

    Volume 1   *Stone Masonry*

    Volume 2   *Brick, Terracotta and Earth*

    Volume 3   *Mortars, Plasters and Renders*

    Volume 4   *Metals*

    Volume 5   *Wood, Glass and Resins*

Breathability

The Need for Old Buildings to Breathe, Information Sheet 4, SPAB

Bricks

Ashurst, John and Nicola, Practical Building Conservation series,
English Heritage Technical Handbooks, Gower Technical Press,
Aldershot, 1988 – Volume 2, *Brick, Terracotta and Earth*

Hammond, Martin, *Bricks and Brickmaking*, Shire Publications,
Princes Risborough, 1981

Lynch, Gerard, *Brickwork, History, Technology and Practice*, Donhead,
Shaftesbury, 1990

Warren, John, *Conservation of Brick*, Butterworth-Heinemann, Oxford, 1998

Ceramic Tiles

Van Lemmen, *Victorian Tiles*, Shire Publications, Princes Risborough, 1981

Damp

The Control of Damp in Old Buildings, Technical Pamphlet 8, SPAB

Dry Stone Walling

Garner, Lawrence, *Dry Stone Walls*, Shire Publications, 1984,
Princes Risborough

The Dry Stone Walling Association of Great Britain produce the following:

    Better Dry Stone Walling, 1991

    Building and Repairing Dry Stone Walls, 1982

    Building Special Features in Dry Stone, 1990

    Creating a Natural Stone Garden, 1996

Earth Buildings

Appropriate Plasters, Renders and Finishes for Cob and Random Stone Walls in Devon, Devon Earth Building Association, July 1993

Ashurst, John and Nicola, Practical Building Conservation Series, English Heritage Technical Handbooks, Gower Technical Press, Aldershot, 1988 – Volume 2 *Brick, Terracotta and Earth*

Earth Structures and Construction in Scotland, Technical Advice Note 6, Historic Scotland, Edinburgh, 1996

Harrison, Ray, *English Heritage Research Transactions*, Volume 3 – *Earth, The Conservation and Repair of Bowhill, Exeter*, James and James Science Publishers, London, July 1999

Keefe, Larry, *The Cob Buildings of Devon, No 1 History, Building Methods and Conservation*, Devon Historic Buildings Trust, January 1992

Keefe, Larry, *The Cob Buildings of Devon, No 2 Repair and Maintenance*, Devon Historic Buildings Trust, September 1993

McCann, John, *Clay and Cob Buildings*, Shire Publications, Princes Risborough, 1983

Pearson, Gordon T, *Conservation of Clay and Chalk Buildings*, Donhead, Shaftesbury, 1992

Terra Britannica, A Celebration of Earthen Structures in Great Britain and Ireland, Edited by John Hurd and Ben Gourley, English Heritage and ICOMOS, UK, 2000

Warren, John, *Conservation of Earth Structures*, Butterworth-Heinemann, Oxford, 1999

Williams-Ellis, Clough, *Building in Cob, Pisé and Stabilized Earth* (1947 Edition), Donhead, Shaftesbury, 1999

Electrics

Electrical Installations, Technical Pamphlet 9, SPAB

Flint

Care and Repair of Flint Walls, Technical Pamphlet 16, SPAB

Floors

Care and Repair of Old Floors, Technical Pamphlet 15, SPAB

Fawcett, Jane, *Historic Floors, Their History and Conservation*, Butterworth-Heinemann, Oxford, 2001

Introduction to Repair of Lime-ash and Plaster Floors, Information Sheet 12, SPAB

How to make Beeswax Polish, Information Sheet 13, SPAB

Patching Old Floorboards, Information Sheet 10, SPAB

Graffiti

The Treatment of Graffiti on Historic Surfaces, Technical Advice Note 18,
    Historic Scotland, Edinburgh, 1999

*Graffiti on Historic Buildings and Monuments: Methods of Removal and
    Prevention*, English Heritage, London, 1999

Glass

Ashurst, John and Nicola, Practical Building Conservation series,
    English Heritage Technical Handbooks, Gower Technical Press,
    Aldershot, 1988 – Volume 5 *Wood, Glass and Resins*

Dodsworth, Roger, *Glass and Glassmaking*, Shire Publications,
    Princes Risborough, 1982

Ironmongery

Monk, Eric, *Keys – Their History and Design*, Shire Publications,
    Princes Risborough

Lime

An Introduction to Building Limes, Information sheet 9, SPAB

Ashurst, John and Nicola, Practical Building Conservation series,
    English Heritage Technical Handbooks, Gower Technical Press,
    Aldershot, 1988 – Volume 3 *Mortars, Plasters and Renders*

Basic Limewash, Information sheet 1, SPAB

Cowper, AD, *Lime and Lime Mortars* (1924 Edition), Donhead, Shaftesbury,
    1998

The English Heritage Directory of Building Limes, Donhead, Shaftesbury, 1997

External Lime Coating on Traditional Buildings, Technical Advice Note 15,
    Historic Scotland, Edinburgh, 2001

Holmes, Stafford and Wingate, Michael, *Building with Lime*,
    Intermediate Technology Publications, London, 1997

Pasley, C.W., *Observation on Limes* (1838 Edition), Donhead, Shaftesbury,
    1997

Preparation and Use of Lime Mortars, Technical Advice Note 1,
    Historic Scotland, Edinburgh, 1995

Schofield, Jane, *Lime in Building: A Practical Guide*, Black Dog Press,
    Crendon, 1995

Vicat, L.J., *Mortars and Cements* (1837 Edition), Donhead, Shaftesbury, 1997

Metals

Ashurst, John and Nicola, Practical Building Conservation series,
    English Heritage Technical Handbooks, Gower Technical Press,
    Aldershot, 1988 – Volume 4 *Metals*

English Heritage Research Transactions, Volume 1: Metals, Edited by
    Jeanne-Marie Teutonico, James and James Science Publishers, London,
    April 1998
Fearn, Jacqueline, *Cast Iron*, Shire Publications, Princes Risborough, 1990,
    revised 2001
Hayman, Richard, *Wrought Iron*, Shire Publications, Princes Risborough, 2000

Paint

*English Heritage Research Transactions, Volume 8: Paint, The Seventeenth-
    Century Decorative Finishes at the Little Castle, Bolsover*, Helen Hughes,
    James and James Science Publishers, London, 2002
Hasluck, Paul N., *House Decoration*, (1897 Edition) Donhead, Shaftesbury,
    2001
Layers of Understanding, edited by Helen Hughes, Donhead, Shaftesbury, 2002

Paint Removal

Removing Paint from Old Buildings, Information Sheet 5, SPAB

Plaster

Bankart, George, *The Art of the Plasterer* (1908 edition), Donhead,
    Shaftesbury, 2002
Conservation of Plasterwork, Technical Advice Note 2, Historic Scotland,
    Edinburgh, 2002
Millar, William, *Plastering Plain and Decorative* (4th Edition facsimile),
    Donhead, Shaftesbury, 2000
Verrall, W., *The Modern Plasterer* (facsimile edition), Donhead, Shaftesbury,
    2000

Pointing

Re-pointing Stone and Brick Walls, Technical Pamphlet 5, SPAB
Tuck Pointing in Practice, Information Sheet 8, SPAB

Roofing

Bennett, Frank and Pinion, Alfred, *Roof Slating and Tiling*, (1935 Edition),
    Donhead, Shaftesbury, 2000
Emerton, Gerald, *The Pattern of Scottish Roofing*, Historic Scotland,
    Edinburgh, 2000
Stone Slate Roofing, English Heritage, London, 1998

Rough-Cast and Harling

External Lime Coating on Traditional Buildings, Technical Advice Note 15,
    Historic Scotland, Edinburgh, 2001
Rough-cast for Historic Buildings, Information Sheet 11, SPAB

Sands

The English Heritage Directory of Building Sands and Aggregates, Donhead,
Shaftesbury, 2000

Scottish Aggregates for Building Conservation, Technical Advice Note 19,
Historic Scotland, Edinburgh, 1999

Slate

Williams, Merfyn, *The Slate Industry*, Shire Publications, Princes Risborough,
1991, 3rd Edition reprinted 2002

Scottish Slate Quarries, Technical Advice Note 21, Historic Scotland,
Edinburgh, 2000

Stone

Ashurst, John and Nicola, Practical Building Conservation series, English
Heritage Technical Handbooks, Gower Technical Press, Aldershot, 1988,
Volume 1 *Stone Masonry*

Building Stone Resources of the United Kingdom, 1:1,000,000 map, Edited by
G.K. Lott, British Geological Survey, 2001

Burn, Robert Scott, *Masonry, Bricklaying and Plastering*, (1871 Edition),
Donhead, Shaftesbury, 2001

Clifton-Taylor, A. and Ireson, A., *English Stone Buildings*, Victor Gollancz,
London, 1994

Dimes, F.G. and Ashurst, J., *Conservation of Building and Decorative Stone*,
Butterworth-Heinemann, Oxford, 1998

English Heritage Research Transactions, Volume 2: Stone, Edited by John Fidler,
James and James Science Publishers, London, 2002

Leary, E., *The Building Limestones of the British Isles*, HMSO, London, 1983

Leary, E., *The Building Sandstones of the British Isles*, HMSO, London, 1986

Quarries of Scotland, Technical Advice Note 12, Historic Scotland,
Edinburgh, 1997

Sustainability

Harland, Edward, *Eco-renovation, The Ecological Home Improvement Guide*,
Green Books, Totness, 1993

Timber decay

English Heritage Research Transactions, Volume 4, Timber, Edited by
Brian Ridout, James and James Science Publishers, London, 2001

Ridout, Brian, *Timber Decay in Buildings: The Conservation Approach to
Treatment*, E & FN Spon, London, 2000

Timber-Framed Buildings

The Repair of Timber Frames and Roofs, Technical Pamphlet 12, SPAB
Panel Infilling to Timber-Framed Buildings, Technical Pamphlet 11, SPAB
First Aid Repair to Traditional Farm Buildings, Information sheet 7, SPAB
Surface Treatment of Timber Framed Houses, Information sheet 3, SPAB

Thatch

English Heritage Research Transactions, Volume 5: Thatching in England 1790–1940, James Moir and John Letts, James and James Science Publishers, London, 1999
English Heritage Research Transactions, Volume 6: Thatching in England 1940–1994, Edited by Jo Cox and John Letts, James and James Science Publishers, London, 2000
Thatch and Thatching Technique, Technical Advice Note 4, Historic Scotland, Edinburgh, 1996
The Archaeology of Scottish Thatch, Technical Advice Note 13, Historic Scotland, Edinburgh, 1998
Thatch and Thatching: A Guidance Note, English Heritage, London, 2000
The Care and Repair of Thatched Roofs, Technical Pamphlet 10, SPAB

Wallpaper

Rosoman, Treve, *London Wallpapers, Their Manufacture and Use 1690–1840*, English Heritage, London, 1992
Saunders, Gill, *Wallpaper in Interior Decoration*, V&A Publications, 2002
Taylor, Clare, *Wallpaper*, Shire Publications, Princes Risborough, 1991

Windows

Performance Standards for Timber Sash and Case Windows, Technical Advice Note 3, Historic Scotland, Edinburgh, 1994
Repair of Wood Windows, Technical Pamphlet 13, SPAB
Framing Options, English Heritage, London:
    1 Draught Proofing; 2 Door and Window furniture; 3 Metal Windows; 4 Timber Sash Windows; 5 Window Comparisons; 7 Energy Savings
The Historical and Technical Development of the Sash and Case Window in Scotland, Research Report, Historic Scotland, Edinburgh, 2001
Conservation and Repair of Sash Windows Practitioners Guide, Historic Scotland, Edinburgh, 2002

Trees

Mynors, Charles, *The Law of Trees, Forests and Hedgerows*, Sweet & Maxwell, London, 2002

The Arboricultural Association produce leaflets on the following topics: No.1 Trees Suitable for Small Gardens; No.2 A Guide to Tree Planting; No.3 Young Tree Maintenance; No.4 Tree Management; No.5 Evergreen Hedges; No.6 Tree Roots; No.7 Thinning Groups of Trees; No.8 Mature Tree Maintenance; No.9 Protection of Trees on Development Sites Part 1; No.10 Protection of Trees on Development Sites Part 2; No.11 Trees: Excavations and Highway Maintenance; No.12 Trees, Subsidence, and other Structural Damage (A Householder's Guide)

Gardens

Harvey, John, *Mediaeval Gardens*, B.T. Batsford, London, 1990
Jacques, David, *Georgian Gardens*, B.T. Batsford, London, 1990
Elliott, Brent, *Victorian Gardens*, B.T. Batsford, London, 1990

Websites

Amenity Societies
Society for the Protection of Ancient Buildings – www.spab.org.uk
Victorian Society – www.victorian-society.org.uk
Georgian Group – www.georgiangroup.org.uk
Twentieth Century Society – www.c20society.demon.co.uk
Ancient Monuments Society – www.ancientmonumentssociety.org.uk

Archaeology
Council for British Archaeology – www.britarch.ac.uk
Institute of Field Archaeologists – www.archaeologists.net

Conservation information
Information about old houses – www.oldhouse.info
Information about heritage – www.heritage-information.org.uk

Government Agencies
English Heritage – www.english-heritage.org.uk
Photographs of listed buildings in England – www.imagesofengland.org.uk
Historic Scotland – www.historic-scotland.gov.uk
Cadw – www.cadw.wales.gov.uk
Environment and Heritage Service – Northern Ireland – www.ehsni.gov.uk
HM Land Registry – www.landreg.gov.uk

Government Departments
Department for Culture, Media and Sport (DCMS) – www.culture.gov.uk
Office of the Deputy Prime Minister (ODPM) – www.odpm.gov.uk

Listed Building Guidance
England – PPG 15: Planning and the Historic Environment –
    www.planning.odpm.gov.uk/ppg
Northern Ireland – Planning Policy Statement 6 –
    www.doeni.gov.uk/planning/Planning_Policy_Statements/Planning_Policy
    _Statement_6/PPS%206.htm

Planning

Planning – A guide for Householders –
  www.planning.odpm.gov.uk/householders/index.htm
A Householder's Planning Guide for the Installation of Satellite Television
  Dishes – www.planning.odpm.gov.uk/satelite/01.htm
The Hedgerow Regulations 1997 –
  www.hmso.gov.uk/si/si1997/97116001.htm

Online library Catalogues and house history research

British Library – www.bl.uk
Public Record Office – www.pro.gov.uk
Royal Institute of British Architects (RIBA) online Library Catalogue –
  www.architecture.com
Local libraries may also have their catalogues available online to members

Professional Bodies

Royal Institute of British Architects (RIBA) – www.architecture.com
Royal Society of Architects in Wales (RSAW) – www.architecture.com
Royal Society of Ulster Architects (RSUA) – www.rsua.org.uk
Royal Town Planning Institute (RTPI) – www.rtpi.org.uk
Royal Incorporation of Architects in Scotland (RIAS) – www.rias.org.uk
Royal Institution of Chartered Surveyors (RICS) – www.rics.org.uk
Institute of Historic Building Conservation (IHBC) – www.ihbc.org.uk
Institution of Structural Engineers (IstructE) – www.istructe.org.uk
Landscape Institute – www.l-i.org.uk
Chartered Institute of Building – www.ciob.org.uk

Building Regulations

Building regulations – www.safety.odpm.gov.uk/bregs/brads.htm
Building standards (Scotland) – www.scotland.gov.uk/build_regs

British Standards

British Standards Institution – www.bsi.org.uk

Health and Safety Issues

Asbestos – www.defra.gov.uk/environment/asbestos/guide/index.htm
Lead paint – www.defra.gov.uk/environment/wotw
Health and Safety Executive (HSE) – www.hse.gov.uk

Party Wall Act

Party Wall Act Explanatory Booklet – www.safety.odpm.gov.uk/bregs/pwact

Sustainability Issues
Greenpeace – www.greenpeace.org

Consumer Safety organisations
Electricity – National Inspection Council for Electrical Installation
Contracting (NICEIC) – www.niceic.org.uk
Council for Registered Gas Installers (CORGI) – www.corgi-gas.com

VAT
HM Customs & Excise – www.hmce.gov.uk

Bats
English Nature – www.english-nature.org.uk
Countryside Council for Wales – www.ccw.gov.uk
Scottish Natural Heritage – www.snh.org.uk
Department of Environment (Northern Ireland) – www.ehsni.gov.uk
The Bat Conservation Trust – www.bats.org.uk

Birds
Royal Society for the Protection of Birds – www.rspb.org.uk

Trees
Arboricultural Association – www.trees.org.uk

Gardens
Royal Horticultural Society (RHS) – www.rhs.org.uk
Garden History Society – www.gardenhistorysociety.org
The Organic Organisation – www.hdra.org.uk
Society of Garden Designers – www.society-of-garden-designers.co.uk

Walls
Dry Stone Walling Association of Great Britain – www.dswa.org.uk

Online Bookshops
RIBA – www.architecture.com
RICS – www.rics.org.uk
The Building Centre – www.buildingcentre.co.uk
Weald & Downland Open Air Museum – www.wealddown.co.uk
Centre for Alternative Technology – www.cat.org.uk

Index